Cute
Knitted
Toys

CONTENTS

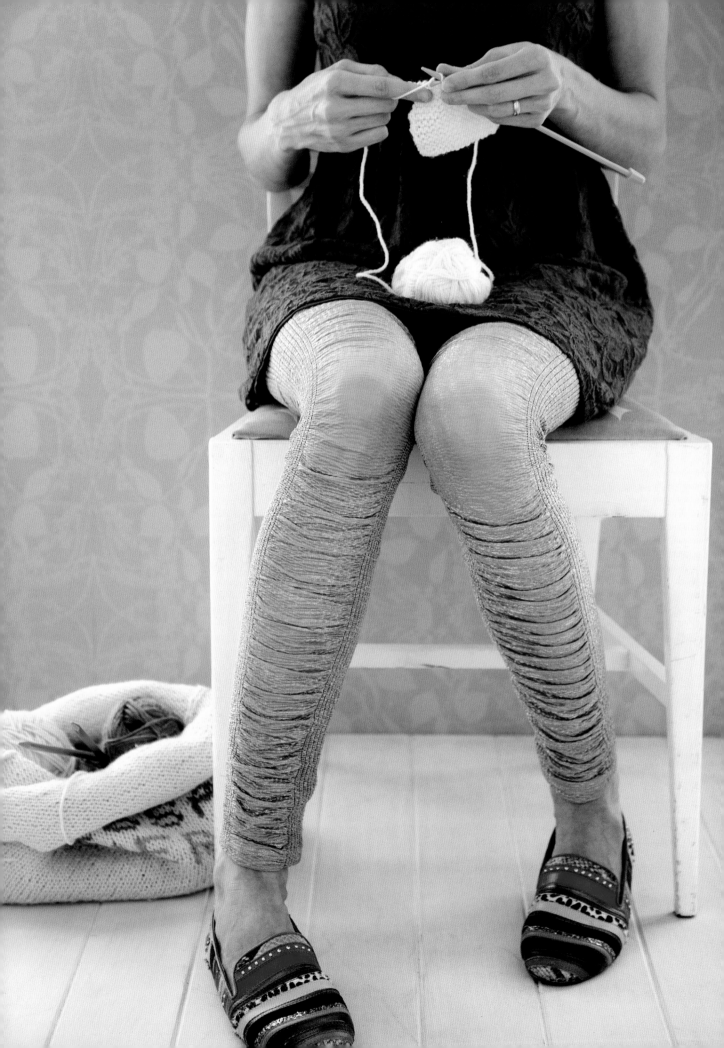

A lot of people say that knitting is making a bit of a comeback – as far as we are concerned, it never left. Knitting is a wonderful craft that allows you to take a humble piece of wool and make virtually anything, anywhere – we created these 20 cuddly creatures on the train, at the beach, with our children in our laps and sometimes even at the dinner table.

All the characters are based on two patterns (see pages 10 and 32) and use a technique called 'Knitting in the Round' (we provide some tips and illustrations on page 113). Starting out can be tricky, but once you get going, all you are doing is knitting in circles. It also means that there is less casting-off and sewing-up when you are done.

You can get the kids involved, too. Teach them to knit with our illustrated guide and easy-to-follow photographs for each pattern. Pieces like Skip the Robot's screen (page 78) or Super Sloth's face (page 64) are knitted flat and would be great starters. Non-knitters can make pompoms for Scaredy Lion's mane (page 52) or Nosey Echidna's many spines (page 22). And everyone can enjoy the poems written for each character. We've tried to keep the patterns as simple as possible. As a general rule, they get a bit trickier as you go. Many of the first patterns don't have arms, as knitting and attaching these can be tricky. If you're a seasoned knitter though, have a look at how we add arms to the Gingerbread Man (page 74) and apply to the pattern of your choice. We also recommend knitting the arms in – if you prefer you can also just bind off the top of the arms and sew them on.

These simple, soft and cute toys are as fun to make as they are to play with.

Happy knitting!

♡ Karla

Karla Courtney
Chief knitter & pattern designer

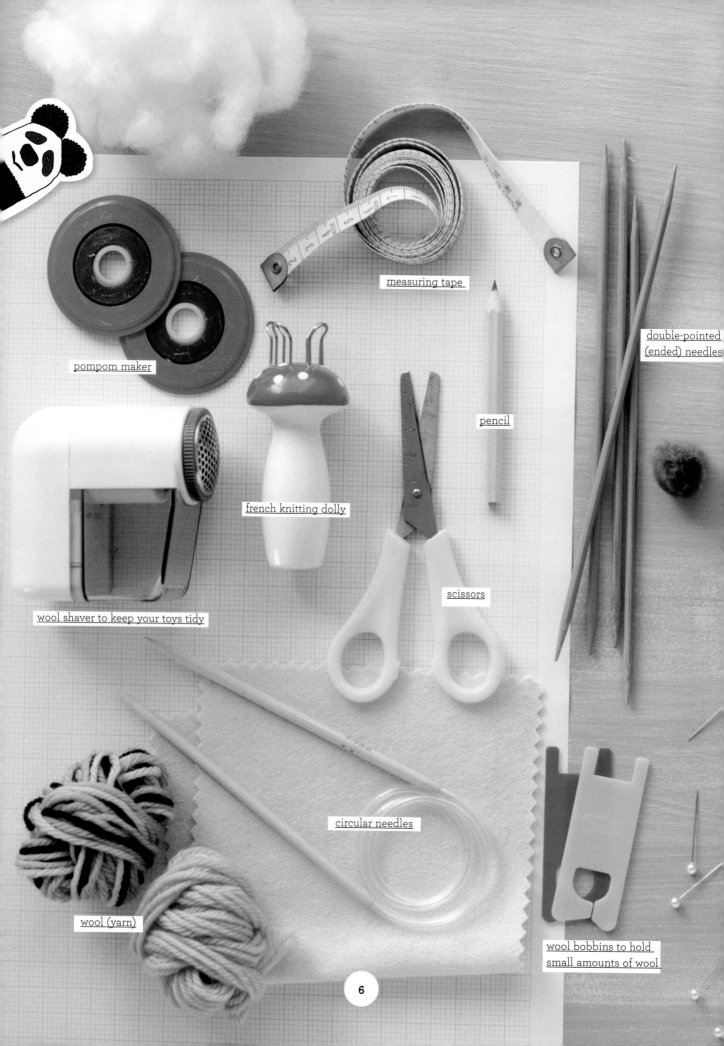

measuring tape

double-pointed (ended) needles

pompom maker

pencil

french knitting dolly

scissors

wool shaver to keep your toys tidy

circular needles

wool (yarn)

wool bobbins to hold small amounts of wool

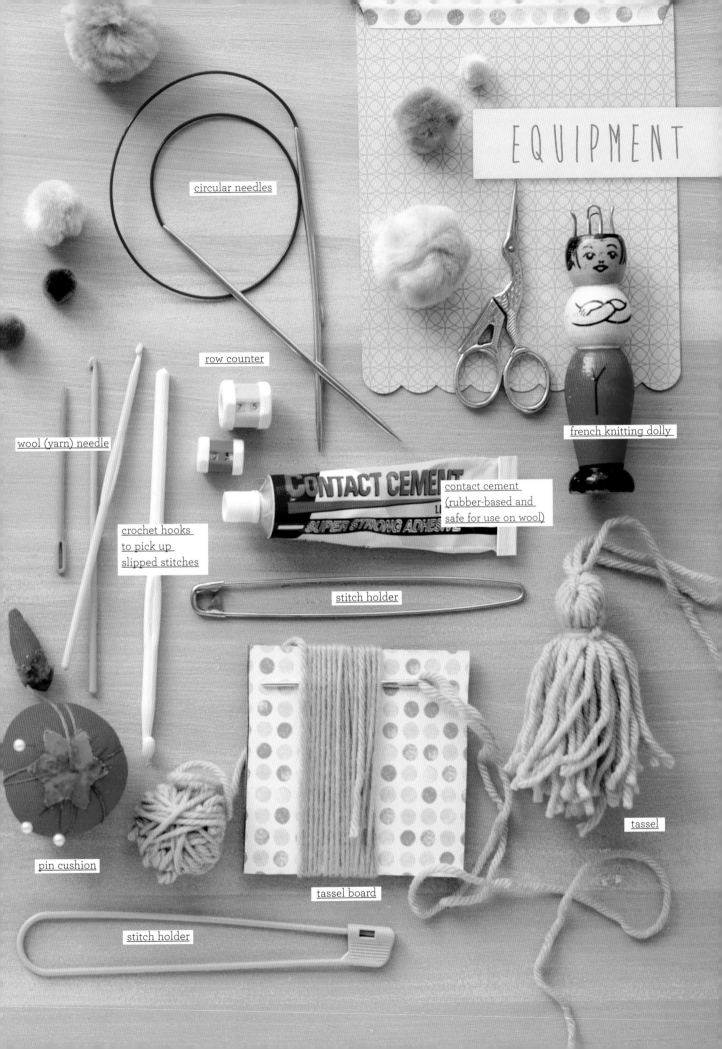

EQUIPMENT

circular needles

row counter

wool (yarn) needle

crochet hooks
to pick up
slipped stitches

french knitting dolly

contact cement
(rubber-based and
safe for use on wool)

CONTACT CEMENT
SUPER STRONG ADHESIVE

stitch holder

pin cushion

tassel board

stitch holder

tassel

TECHNICAL NOTES

Safety notes

Many of the patterns in this book include pompoms and knitted embellishments. If you are planning on giving these toys to a young child under the age of three you need to take great care in fastening these items. We provide some tips for fastening securely on page 116 *'sewing onto your work'* and page 117 *'sewing on pompoms and tassels'*.

We used a tweed wool to knit the sloth. Some tweed wools may have small bits that can be easily picked off and swallowed. We do not recommend using any tweed or other textured wools if you are giving the toy to children under the age of three.

Tension

Tension generally refers to how tightly you are working with your wool to knit your stitches. Tension is especially important when knitting garments, as this can alter the size and shape. Tension is less important for these toys – most important is that you feel comfortable with how you are knitting and that you aren't finding your stitches too tight or loose to work with. Most wool will indicate a recommended tension based on a certain needle size. If you wish, you can use this as a guide.

The animals in this book should range in height/length from 26cm to 32cm depending on the specific wool that you use and your own tension.

Wool

We have used a variety of colours and textures of wools in this book – all are 8-ply.

Some toys require you to change colours – not all 8-ply wools have the same texture and some brands and batches will be thicker than others. For a consistent tension, use wools of the same brand and variety for each toy.

We have chosen our own wool colours for the toys as a guideline – some toys, such as the zebra and giraffe, rely on their colours to tell people what they are. You can use our colours as a guide and substitute as you see fit. The most important thing, however, is that your wool is 8-ply – and that you like it!

Stuffing

All our toys require stuffing to make them soft and cuddly. Most craft and departments stores will stock stuffing that is suitable. We used around 75-100g of acrylic stuffing per toy.

It is up to you how exactly you want to stuff your toy – as a guideline you don't want to stuff it so full that the stitches spilt. Stuff enough so that it feels springy without being too tight.

Most of our patterns recommend that you stuff as you go. This makes it easier to get a good and consistent shape. It can also be difficult to stuff down to the bottom of your toy when you are at the top of your work.

Washing instructions

Hand-wash your toy using cool water and detergent that is suited to wools. Gently wring it out to remove the excess water from the stuffing. Lay it to dry on an airer. Do not leave the toy soaking in water. Take extra care with the pompoms and tassels.

Needle sizes

The size of the needles refers to the diameter. All of the patterns in this book require 4mm double-pointed needles. The shark also requires long or circular 3.25mm needles to knit his fine teeth.

American	English	Metric (mm)
0	14	2
1	13	2.25
2	12	2.75
3	10	3.25
4	–	3.5
5	9	3.75
6	8	4
7	7	4.5
8	6	5
9	5	5.5
10	4	6
10.5	3	6.5
11	0	8
13	00	9

Reading our patterns

We have created two master body patterns that form the base of all the patterns in this book. See page 10 for the Basic Body shape, and page 32 for the Body with Legs. Each master pattern indicates which toys can be made using these patterns. Silverback Gorilla, Napoleon Penguin and Sleepy Shark are a bit more difficult than the basic shapes and follow their own patterns.

Using glue on wool

As a shortcut you can use hot glue or contact cement to attach wool embellishments, however, this is not as effective as sewing them on and is not recommended if giving to a child. Contact cement does not cause any burning reaction with cotton/wool. Do not use super glue, as this causes a chemical reaction with wool and cotton fibres. Personal care should be taken when using glue to adhere embellishments to the wool so as not to burn yourself, or stick yourself to the toy!

Terms and abbreviations

When you are reading a knitting pattern, you will see a lot of abbreviations – here are the standard terms and abbreviations used in our book:

Main (M) colour This refers to the prominent colour of wool used in your project

Contrast (C) colour This refers to the secondary colour of wool that is used in your project

Garter st Knit every row

Inc 1 Increase a stitch. (Inc 2 means increase two stitches)

K Knit, (K2) means knit two stitches. K1 row means knit the entire row

K2 tog Knit 2 stitches together at the same time. This is a common decrease stitch that creates a slant to the right of the pattern

P Purl, (P2) means purl two stitches. P1 row means purl the entire row

Rnd Round, refers to a complete round of stitches on the needles

S1 Slip one stitch onto the opposite needle without knitting it

S1k1 psso Slip one stitch, knit one stitch, pass the slipped stitch over. This is a common decrease stitch that creates a slant to the left

St Stitch

Sts Stitches

Stocking st Knit one row, purl one row

* to **, repeat the process in between these symbols as many times as the pattern requires.

BASIC BODY

Here's a simple shape to get you started – this is a basic tube that you can knit entirely in the round using four 4mm double-pointed needles, so there is very minimal making-up when you are done.

Read this pattern carefully and familiarise yourself with the steps before you select your animal. The four animals that use this body pattern will have a few additional steps to transform it into that animal shape.

We recommend that you have your stuffing on hand and stuff the body as you go.

If you are a bit more comfortable with knitting, use this pattern as a base and think of what other animals you can make on your own – think about different colour combinations, embroidery styles and ways you can place the pompoms!

Animals that use this pattern as a base

Wobbly Wombat (page 14)

Cute Panda (page 18)

Nosey Echidna (page 22)

Hipster Owl (page 26)

Materials needed

4 x double-pointed 4mm needles

Wool needle

Scissors

Wool (100g main colour; 50g contrast colour)

Stuffing

Skills needed

Casting on

Knit stitch (K)

Knitting in the round

Increasing stitches (Inc 1)

Decreasing stitches (K2 tog)

Changing colours

If you are unfamiliar with any of these materials or skills, turn to pages 6 and 112 for details.

Once you are familiar with how to knit this basic shape, try one of the animals on pages 14-26.

Body

Using the (M) wool, cast 8 sts onto a 4mm double-pointed needle (pic a).

Take these 8 sts and distribute them across 3 double-pointed needles (2-4-2) (pic b).

Work 1 rnd in knit stitch. Continue in k for the rest of the body.

2nd rnd Inc 1 in every st, (4-8-4) 16 sts.

Work 1 rnd.

4th rnd: *K1, inc 1**, repeat *to** for the entire rnd, (6-12-6) 24 sts.

Work 1 rnd.

6th rnd: *K2, inc 1**, repeat *to** for the entire rnd, (8-16-8) 32 sts.

Note: *what you are doing is increasing the number of stitches on the two needles with the lesser number by 2 stitches, and on the needle with the greater number of stitches by 4 stitches - 8 stitches every other round. It is important that you follow this pattern, paying close attention to the number of stitches between each increased stitch, as indicated in the pattern, as this is what creates a clean diagonal line up your work.*

Work 1 rnd.

8th rnd *K3, inc 1**, repeat *to** for the entire rnd, (10-20-10) 40 sts.

Work 1 rnd.

10th rnd *K4, inc 1**, repeat *to** for the entire rnd, (12-24-12) 48 sts.

Work 1 rnd.

12th rnd: *K5, inc 1**, repeat *to** for the entire rnd, (14-28-14) 56 sts.

Work 1 rnd.

Continue to work these 56 sts for 56 more rnds (pic c).

70th rnd: Switch to the C wool. (See page 116 for tips on joining a new colour) (pic d).

Work 24 rnds with C.

Begin decrease to form head

95th rnd *K5, k2 tog**, repeat *to** for the entire rnd, (12-24-12) 48 sts.

Work 1 rnd.

97th rnd: *K4, k2 tog**, repeat *to** for the entire rnd, (10-20-10) 40 sts.

Work 1 rnd.

99th rnd: *K3, k2 tog**, repeat *to** for the entire rnd, (8-16-8) 32 sts.

Work 1 rnd.

101st rnd *K2, k2 tog**, repeat *to** for the entire rnd, (6-12-6) 24 sts.

Work 1 rnd.

103rd rnd *K1, k2 tog**, repeat *to** for the entire rnd, (4-8-4) 16 sts.

Work 1 rnd.

105th rnd K2 tog for the entire rnd, (2-4-2) 8 sts.

You have finished the body. Ensure the body is stuffed to how firm or soft you want it before you close it up. See page 8 for tips on stuffing.

Cut the wool, leaving a minimum of 16cm wool hanging. Thread a wool needle and pull the wool through the 8 sts, removing them from the needle as you go (pic e).

Pull the loose end tightly to close the stitches (pic f).

Make up

Hide any loose wool ends from casting on and finishing inside the body (see '*hiding wool inside of body*' page 116 for instructions).

Cast on 8 stitches (a), then distribute them across 3 double-pointed needles in a triangular pattern (b). Follow the pattern to increase from 8 to 56 stitches (c), then work these stitches for 56 rows. Change to the contrast colour (d) and work 24 more rows, stuffing the body as you go. Then, with your working end cut, pull it though the remaining stitches with a wool needle (e, f).

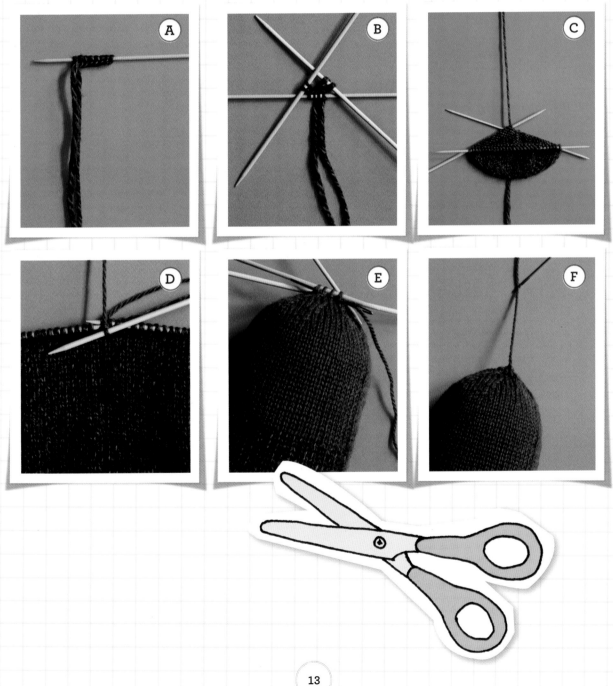

WOBBLY WOMBAT

A wombat's claws are strong though small, This wombat has no claws at all! She has great sense of sight and sound, But needs help standing on the ground.

Materials needed

4 x double-pointed 4mm needles
Wool (100g greyish brown for main colour; 50g dark grey for contrast colour; skein of black for the eye embroidery and pompom nose; small amount of white for eye detail)
Wool needle
Pompom maker
Scissors
Stuffing

Skills needed

Casting on
Knit stitch (K)
Increasing stitches (Inc 1)
Decreasing stitches (K2 tog, s1k1 psso)
Casting off
Knitting in the round
Changing colours
Duplicate stitch embroidery
Pompom making
Sewing

If you are unfamiliar with any of these skills or materials, turn to pages 6 and 12 for details.

Tip

We've kept this wombat as simple as possible, but if you're a bit more comfortable with knitting, you can follow the pattern for the 'leg' on the Body with Legs pattern (page 32) with the following modification: once you've finished the increase and have 24 stitches, work for 4 rnds instead of 24. Use the 3-needle joining and binding technique (page 115) to finish off, then attach to the bottom of the body. Follow the instructions to make 4 legs for the wombat.

Ears

The ears are knitted flat (using knit stitch for each row creates what's known as garter stitch). You only need 2 x 4mm needles.

Cast on 10 sts with the greyish brown main (M) wool. Ensure you leave at least 12cm wool hanging to finish the ears and sew them onto the wombat's body.

*K1 row

2nd row: S1k1 psso, k to last 2 sts, k2 tog** (8 sts).

Repeat * to ** until 2 stitches remain.

9th row: K1 row.

10th row: Pass 1 st over the other, (1 st remains).

Cut the wool, leaving around 10cm. Thread a wool needle, and pull the loose end through the remaining stitch then hide this end away. (See '*weaving method*' page 116 for instructions on how to hide wool ends inside the body.)

Pinch the ear together to create a more pointed and angled wombat's ear.

Lay the ear flat (pic b), thread a wool needle with the leftover wool from the cast on and use this to sew the two bottom corners together (pic c). Pull this tightly and then remove the needle and put aside. When you attach the ears to the body use this wool end.

Repeat this process for the 2nd ear.

Nose

Using a pompom maker with a 60-70mm diameter (centre hole will be around 10mm) and the black wool, make a black pompom. Refer to instructions '*making a pompom*' on page 114.

Body

Follow the instructions for the Basic Body shape on page 10, with the following modifications:

Stop after finishing the 94th rnd, and before you begin to decrease to form the head, so that you can add the eyes (pic d).

Do not stuff under the area where you will be adding the eyes as it will be more difficult to work with.

To create the eyes follow the grid on page 17, using duplicate stitch (see '*embroidery stitches*' page 114) and the black and white wools.

Continue with the decrease to shape and finish the head as per the Basic Body shape instructions. Ensure the body is stuffed to how firm or soft you want it before you close it up. See page 8 for tips on stuffing.

Make up

Hide any loose wool ends at the top and bottom of the body (see '*hiding wool inside of body*' page 116 for instructions).

Sew the pompom nose onto the face (see '*sewing on pompoms and tassels*' page 117).

Wombat Eye Grid

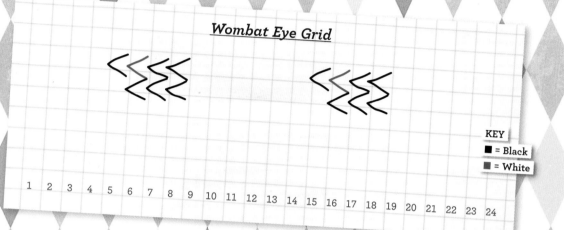

KEY
■ = Black
■ = White

1 2 3 4 5 6 7 8 9 10 11 12 13 14 15 16 17 18 19 20 21 22 23 24

A

B

C

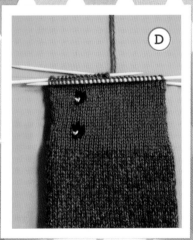

D

These steps show how to pinch the wombat's ear and sew it together so it has a nice shape (b, c). Also take note of where the wombat's eyes are positioned (d); they are embroidered onto the wombat before stuffing the top and closing.

CUTE PANDA

Panda's more than a cute face, She climbs a tree with strength
and grace, And when she's not chewing bamboo
She's working hard on her Kung Fu.

Materials needed

4 x double-pointed 4mm needles

Wool (100g white for main colour; 50g black for
contrast colour)

Wool needle

Pompom maker

Scissors

Stuffing

Skills needed

Casting on

Knit stitch (K)

Increasing stitches (Inc 1)

Decreasing stitches (K2 tog, s1k1 psso)

Casting off

Knitting in the round

Changing colours

Duplicate stitch embroidery

Pompom making

*If you are unfamiliar with any of these skills
or materials, turn to pages 6 and 112 for
details.*

Tip

If you're comfortable with knitting and
would like the panda to have legs, follow
the Body with Legs pattern (page 32) with
the following modifications: after you've
finished the legs, work 16 more rows using
the white wool. Switch to black wool for
the next 24 rows, then switch back to white
wool, and continue with the basic body
pattern. If you want upper limbs, follow the
'arms' instructions for the Gingerbread Man
(page 74) using black wool.

Ears

Using a pompom maker with a 60-70mm diameter (centre hole will be around 10mm) and the black wool, make 2 black pompoms. Refer to the pompom instructions on page 114.

Nose

The nose is knitted flat (using knit stitch for each row creates what's known as garter stitch). You only need 2 x 4mm needles. Leave at least 12cm of wool hanging after casting on as you will use this later to sew the nose onto the face.

Cast on 6 sts with the black wool.

K3 rows.

4th row: S1k1 psso, k to last 2 sts, k2 tog, (4 sts).

K2 rows.

Cast off.

Cut the wool, leaving around 10cm. With a wool needle put the loose end through the remaining stitch and then hide this end (see 'weaving method' instructions on page 116).

Body

Follow the Basic Body shape instructions on page 10, with the following modifications:

46th rnd: Join to black wool (see 'joining new wool or changing colours' page 116).

Work 23 rnds black.

70th rnd: Join to white wool.

Work 23 rnds white.

Stop after finishing the 94th rnd and before you begin to decrease to form the head so you can add the eyes and mouth (pic b).

To create the eyes follow the grid on page 21, using

duplicate stitch (see 'embroidery stitches' page 114) and the black and white wools.

To create the mouth, use one large loose straight stitch with a couching stitch to secure it (see 'embroidery stitches' page 114) , following the grid pattern.

Continue with the decrease to shape and finish the head as per the Basic Body instructions. Ensure the body is stuffed to how firm or soft you want it before you close it up. See page 8 for tips on stuffing.

Make up

Hide any loose wool ends at the top and bottom of the body. See 'hiding wool inside of body' page 116 for instructions.

Once you have closed the head, attach the pompom ears securely to the body (see 'sewing on pompoms and tassels' page 117).

Sew the nose on securely (see 'sewing onto your work' page 116).

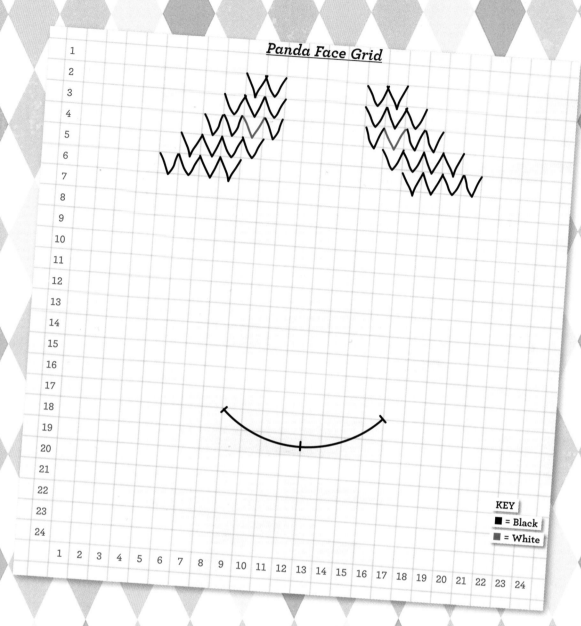

Panda Face Grid

KEY

■ = Black
■ = White

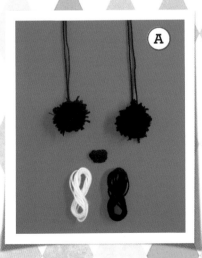

A

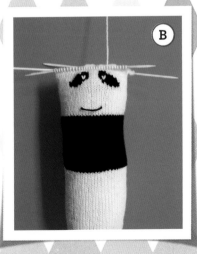

B

Even though he looks quite different, the panda doesn't have many modifications, apart from the pompom ears, knitted nose, black stripe and embroidered face...none of which are too difficult.

NOSEY ECHIDNA

It's clear our friend has many spines, But did you know that
when he dines, He has no teeth! Though he has a snout,
A part he cannot eat without.

Materials needed

4 x double-pointed 4mm needles
Wool (100g yellow for main colour; 50g dark
brown for contrast colour; skein of blue for eyes)
Wool needle
Pompom maker
Scissors
Stuffing

Skills needed

Casting on
Knit stitch (K)
Increasing stitches (Inc 1)
Decreasing stitches (K2 tog, s1k1 psso)
Casting off
Knitting in the round
Changing colours
Weaving method to hide wool ends
Pompom making
Sewing

*If you are unfamiliar with any of these materials
or skills, turn to pages 6 and 112 for details.*

Tip

The trickiest part about the echidna is
the long, skinny snout. It can be difficult
working with only eight stitches on these
needles. However, just work slowly, paying
close attention so you don't twist the
needles or drop a stitch. If you're finding it
too difficult, replace it with a thick brown
cord (available from craft stores), or cut a
finger off a small child's woollen glove and
attach it to the body.

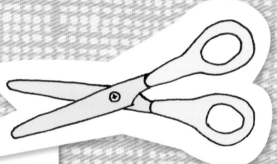

Spines

Echidnas' backs are covered with spines – we made 21 pompoms to cover the back of the echidna, combining yellow and brown wools (pics a, b, c), and using a pompom maker with a 60-70mm diameter (centre hole will be around 10mm). See page 114 for pompom making instructions.

Body

Follow the instructions of the Basic Body shape on page 10, with the following modifications:

Begin to decrease on the 82nd rnd (after working 12 rnds with dark brown wool).

Stop once you reach 8-16-8 sts. Make sure you haven't stuffed right to the top as you will need room for sewing.

Using the blue wool, sew on the eyes using 2 straight stitches (see '*embroidery stitches*' page 114) following the grid below (pic d).

Once you have decreased to 8 sts, work these for 12 rnds to create the echidna's snout (pic e).

Once you are finished these 12 rnds, cut and thread the wool through the 8 sts using a wool needle.

Ensure the body is stuffed to how firm or soft you want it before you close it up. See page 8 for tips on stuffing.

Make up

Hide any loose wool ends at the base and snout (see '*hiding wool inside of body*' page 116 for instructions).

To finish echidna, sew the pompom spines to his back (pic f). We used a configuration of 5 rows, starting with 1 row down the spine of his back, followed by 2 rows of 4 on either side (see '*sewing on pompoms and tassels*' page 117).

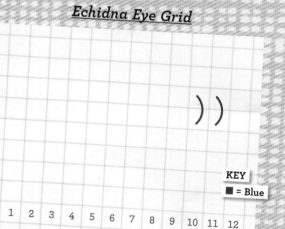

Echidna Eye Grid

))

KEY

■ = Blue

1 2 3 4 5 6 7 8 9 10 11 12

Using the pompom makers, make the echidna's spikes. We've combined yellow and brown wool, using more brown and less yellow wool, to give the spikes a nice colour (a, b). Use the grid (page 24) as a guide and add the eyes (d) before beginning to knit the snout (e). Attach the pompoms securely (f) then, if you like, trim them a little shorter so they stand up more like spikes.

HIPSTER OWL

What song is this? "You wouldn't know, I heard it at
a secret show", His need for specs is not genetic
He wears them for their cool aesthetic.

Materials needed

4 x double-pointed 4mm needles
Wool (100g turquoise for main colour; 50g red
for contrast colour; 25g each of yellow, orange
and black for wings, eyes, beak and glasses)
Wool needle
Stitch holder
Scissors
Stuffing

Skills needed

Casting on
Knit stitch (K)
Increasing stitches (Inc 1)
Decreasing stitches (K2 tog, s1k1 psso)
Casting off
Knitting in the round
Transferring stitches to and from a stitch holder
Changing colours
Duplicate stitch embroidery
Sewing

*If you are unfamiliar with any of these materials
or skills, turn to pages 6 and 112 for details.*

Tip

Hipster Owl doesn't need glasses. You can
add these if you want him to look extra cool;
just follow the instructions on the grid on
page 29. The owl is also quite long; if you'd
prefer a shorter, more rounded owl, work
the main colour of the body for 28 rounds
instead of 56. Use whatever colours you
like...this cool owl would look hip in any of
your favourite colours.

Eyes

The eyes are knitted flat (using knit stitch for each row creates what's known as garter stitch). You only need 2 x 4mm needles.

Cast on 4 sts with the yellow wool, leaving at least 12cm wool hanging so you have enough to sew the eyes onto the face.

Knit 1 row.

Begin increase

2nd row: K1, inc 1, inc 1, k1, (6 sts).

Knit 1 row.

4th row: K1, inc 1, k2, inc 1, k1, (8 sts).

Knit 3 rows.

Begin decrease

8th row: K1, s1k1 psso, k2, k2 tog, k1, (6 sts).

Knit 1 row.

10th row: K1, s1k1 psso, k2 tog, k1, (4 sts).

Cast off. Hide the loose wool end (see *'weaving method'* page 116 for instructions).

Take the black wool and, following the grid on page 29, sew on the eyes using 2 straight stitches (see *'embroidery stitches'* page 114).

Repeat for the 2nd eye.

Large wing pieces

The wings are also knitted flat, using k stitch for each row to create a garter stitch. You only need 2 x 4mm needles.

Cast on 8 sts with the yellow wool leaving at least 16cm wool hanging so you have enough to sew the wings onto the body.

K1 row.

2nd row: K1, inc 1, k to last 2 sts, inc 1, k1, (10 sts).

Work these 10 sts for 23 rows.

Begin decrease

*K1 row.

27th row: S1k1 psso, k to last 2 sts, k2 tog, k1**, (8 sts).

Repeat * to ** until there are 2 stitches remaining.

36th row: Pass 1 st over the other.

Cut the wool, leaving around 10cm. Thread a wool needle and pull the loose end through the remaining stitch and hide the end (see *'weaving method'* page 116 for instructions).

Repeat for the 2nd wing.

Small wing pieces

Repeat as per large wing, except only k for 11 rows instead of 23.

Make 4 small wing pieces, 2 x black and 2 x orange.

Beak

The beak is also knitted flat, using knit stitch for each row to create a garter stitch. You only need 2 x 4mm needles.

Cast on 8 sts with the orange wool, leaving at least 12cm wool hanging so you have enough to sew the beak onto the face.

*Knit 1 row.

2nd row: S1k1 psso, k to remaining 2 sts, k2 tog**, (6 sts).

Repeat * to ** until 2 stitches remain.

Knit 1 row.

9th row: Cut the wool, leaving around 10cm. Hide the loose wool end (see *'weaving method'* page 116 for instructions).

(instructions continue page 30)

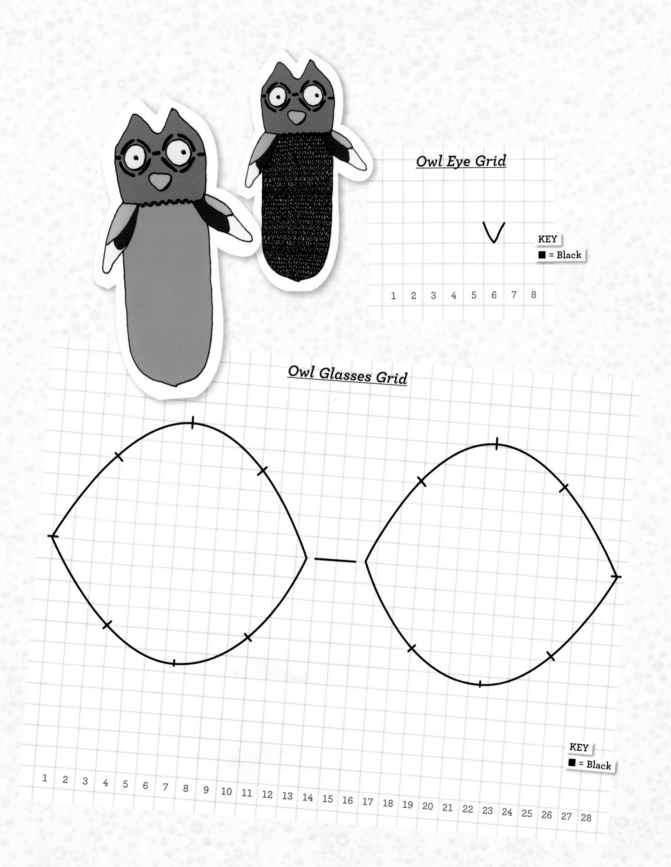

Owl Eye Grid

KEY
■ = Black

1 2 3 4 5 6 7 8

Owl Glasses Grid

KEY
■ = Black

1 2 3 4 5 6 7 8 9 10 11 12 13 14 15 16 17 18 19 20 21 22 23 24 25 26 27 28

(instructions continue from page 28)

Body

Follow the instructions for the Basic Body shape on page 10, with the following modifications:

Stop after finishing the 94th rnd. Make sure that you haven't stuffed right to the top as you will need room for sewing.

Add the embroidered glasses, using large straight stitches with couching stitches to secure (see '*embroidery stitches*' page 114), following the grid on page 29 (pics a, b).

Ensure the body is stuffed to how firm or soft you want it before beginning the ears. See page 8 for tips on stuffing.

Shaping the ears

Take 28 sts (14 from the left front and 14 from the left back needles and place them on a stitch holder (pic c). Reconfigure the 3 needles (7-14-7), with the 14-st needle across the front (pic d).

95th rnd: *K5, k2 tog**, repeat *to** for the entire rnd, (6-12-6) 24 sts.

Work 1 rnd.

97th rnd: *K4, k2 tog**, repeat *to** for the entire rnd, (5-10-5) 20 sts.

Work 1 rnd.

99th rnd: *K3, k2 tog**, repeat *to** for the entire rnd, (4-8-4) 16 sts.

Work 1 rnd.

101st rnd: *K2, k2 tog**, repeat *to** for the entire rnd, (3-6-3) 12 sts.

Work 1 rnd.

103rd rnd: *K1, k2 tog**, repeat *to** for the entire rnd, (2-4-2) 8 sts.

Work 1 rnd.

105th rnd: K2 tog for the entire rnd, (1-2-1) 4 sts.

Cut the wool leaving around 10cm. Thread a wool needle and pass it through these 4 sts as you pull them off the needle.

Remove the stitches from the stitch holder and place them across 3 needles (7-14-7) as per the first ear.

Repeat these steps for the 2nd ear.

Ensure the ears are stuffed to how firm or soft you want them before finishing the second ear.

Make up

Hide any loose wool ends at the top and bottom of the body (see '*hiding wool inside of body*' page 116 for instructions).

Sew the beak on securely (see '*sewing onto your work*' page 116).

Arrange the wing pieces into a wing shape (pic e); sew pieces together (pic f). Sew wings, beak and eyes onto the body.

Sew the small gap between the ears closed (refer to pictures h and i on page 35 - while these pictures show sewing the gap between the legs, it is similar to sewing up between the ears).

Pictures e, f, show how the wing pieces are arranged and sewn together. When shaping the glasses (a, b), leave enough space so that they fit around the eyes. Pictures c, d, show how the needles should be configured to shape the individual ears.

BODY WITH LEGS

The 'body with legs' pattern forms the base of the next 14 animals in this book. There are a few new, though not too hard, techniques to learn, but these will allow you to create other shapes and characters.

Animals that use this pattern as a base

Hungry Bunny (page 36)
Lazy Koala (page 40)
Crested Cockatoo (page 44)
Zippy Zebra (page 48)
Scaredy Lion (page 52)
Flying Unicorn (page 56)

Using 3-needle joining to attach legs and arms

(see page 114 for instructions)
Cool Cat (page 60)
Super Sloth (page 64)
Rainbow Elephant (page 70)
Gingerbread Man (page 74)

Using 3-needle joining and binding to create an edge

(see page 115 for instructions)
Skip the Robot (page 78)
Diplodocus Dino (page 84)
Baby Giraffe (page 88)

Materials needed

4 x double-pointed 4mm needles
Stitch holder
Wool needle
Scissors
Wool (100g main colour; 50g contrast colour)
Stuffing

Skills needed

Casting on
Knit stitch (K)
Knitting in the round
Increasing stitches (Inc 1)
Decreasing stitches (K2 tog)
Changing colours
Transferring stitches to and from a stitch holder

If you are unfamiliar with any of these materials or skills, turn to pages 6 and 112 for details.

Like the basic body shape, this pattern is also knitted entirely in the round using four 4mm double-pointed needles, so there is very minimal making-up when you are done. Read the pattern carefully, and familiarise yourself with the steps before you start the project. We recommend that you have your stuffing on hand and to stuff the body as you go.

Legs

Cast on 4 sts onto a 4mm double-pointed needle using the contrast (C) wool (pic a).

Next row: Inc 1 in every st, (8 sts).

Take these 8 sts and distribute them across 3 double-pointed needles, (2-4-2) (pic b).

Work 1 rnd.

3rd rnd: *K1, inc 1**, repeat *to** for the entire rnd, (3-6-3) 12 sts.

Work 1 rnd.

5th rnd: *K2, inc 1**, repeat *to** for the entire rnd, (4-8-4) 16 sts.

Note: *what you are doing is increasing the needles with the lesser number of stitches by 1 st and the needle with the greater number of stitches by 2 sts every other rnd – 4 sts each time. On the needles with fewer stitches, you are increasing the last stitch, and on the remaining needle, you are increasing 1 middle stitch and then the last stitch. It's important to follow this pattern, as it will make a clean diagonal line up your work.*

7th rnd: *K3, inc 1**, repeat *to** for the entire rnd, (5-10-5) 20 sts.

Work 1 rnd.

9th rnd: *K4, inc 1**, repeat *to** for the entire rnd, (6-12-6) 24 sts.

Work 1 rnd.

Switch to the main (M) wool colour (see '*joining new wool or changing colours*' page 116 for tips on how to switch colours).

Work 24 rnds.

Take this work and place it on a stitch holder (see '*using a stitch holder*' page 116) (pic c).

You have finished one leg.

Repeat this process to create a 2nd leg. Once complete, leave the 2nd leg on the needles.

Body

Join the two legs together on 3 x 4mm double-pointed needles, with the stitches split 12-24-12 across the needles (pics d, e).

Work 64 rnds.

Begin decrease to form head

65th rnd: *K4, k2 tog**, repeat *to** for the entire rnd, (10-20-10) 40 sts.

Work 1 rnd.

67th rnd: *K3, k2 tog**, repeat *to** for the entire rnd, (8-16-8) 32 sts.

Work 1 rnd.

67th rnd: *K2, k2 tog**, repeat *to** for the entire rnd, (6-12-6) 24 sts.

Work 1 rnd.

71st rnd: *K1, k2 tog**, repeat *to** for the entire rnd, (4-8-4) 16 sts.

Work 1 rnd.

73rd rnd: K2 tog for the entire rnd, (2-4-2) 8 sts.

The body is now finished. Ensure the body is stuffed to how firm or soft you want it before you close it up. See page 8 for tips on stuffing.

Cut the wool leaving around 16cm hanging. Thread a wool needle and pass it through these 8 sts as you pull them off the needle. Pull the loose end tightly to close the stitches (pics f, g).

Make up

Hide any loose wool ends from casting on and finishing inside the body (see '*hiding wool inside of body*' page 116 for instructions).

Sew the small gap between the legs closed (pics h, i).

The trickiest part when knitting the body with legs is getting started; these steps show how the eight stitches are distributed across the three needles (b). As you increase, it becomes much easier to work with the three needles. Pay close attention to the position of the needles when joining the legs together to form the body (d, e).

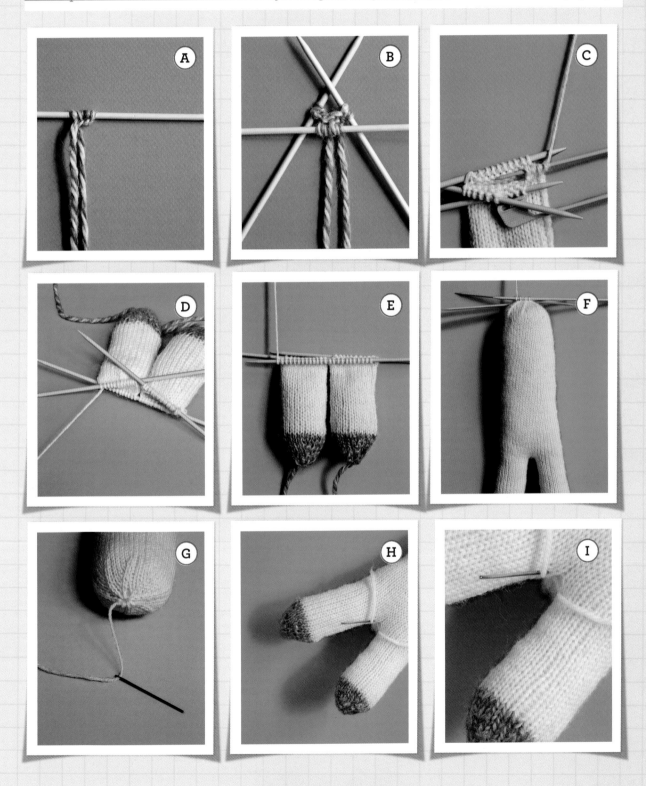

HUNGRY BUNNY

The bunny's hop is his great merit, But all this guy
wants is a carrot, Pat his back and watch him flee,
He'll be back when he's hungry.

Materials needed

4 x double-pointed 4mm needles
Wool (100g off-white for main colour; 50g grey
for contrast colour; small skeins of blue and
orange for the nose and eyes)
Scissors
Stitch holder
Wool needle
Pompom maker
Stuffing
Lightly dampened towel or cloth
Iron

Tip

To keep the pattern simpler, the arms
have been left off the bunny. If you'd
like the bunny to have arms, follow the
'arms' instructions for the Gingerbread Man
(page 74) using grey wool for the contrast
colour and white wool as the main colour.

Skills needed

Casting on
Casting off
Knit stitch (K)
Purl stitch (P)
Knitting in the round
Increasing stitches (Inc 1)
Decreasing stitches (K2 tog, s1k1 psso)
Duplicate stitch embroidery
Knitting with two colours side-by-side
Changing colours
Transferring stitches to and from a stitch holder
Mattress stitch
Sewing

*If you are unfamiliar with any of these materials
or skills, turn to pages 6 and 112 for details.*

Tail

Using a pompom maker with a 60-70mm diameter (centre hole will be around 10mm) and the grey contrast wool, make a grey pompom. Refer to instructions 'making a pompom' on page 114.

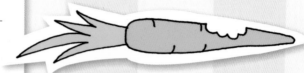

Ears

The ears are knitted flat, using knit and purl stitches on alternating rows (known as stocking stitch). You only need 2 x 4mm needles.

You will knit using 2 different colours on 1 needle to create the white front and the grey inside of the ear. This means you won't have to sew the ears pieces together later, and ensures both sides are identical, which makes it easier to make up.

Cast on 8 sts with the main (M) wool (pic b). Using the grey contrast (C) wool, cast on 8 sts (pic b). **Note:** wrap this strand around the white M strand before joining the 2 wools. See page 114 for instructions on 'knitting with 2 colours side-by-side' (pic c).

Next row: *P to end, switching from C to M where the divide occurs. Continue to do this for the rest of the ear.

2nd row: K to end.

3rd row: P to end.**

Repeat * to ** until you have 7 rows.

Begin decrease

8th row: *With the right side facing, s1k1 psso, k to last 2 sts, k2 tog, (14 sts - 7 main, 7 contrast).

Work 7 more rows stocking st.**

Repeat * to ** until 6 sts (3 M, 3 C) remain. Cast off.

Cut the M wool leaving at least 30cm to sew the edge together.

Cut the C wool leaving around 50mm so that you can hide it inside the folded ear.

Repeat this process for the 2nd ear. Put aside to attach to the body.

Body

Follow the instructions for the Body with Legs pattern on page 32, with the following modifications:

Stop when you have completed the 64th body rnd. Make sure you haven't stuffed right to the top as you will need room for sewing (pic d).

Sew on the eyes and nose using duplicate stitch for the eyes and straight stitch for the nose (see 'embroidery stitches' page 114), following the grid on page 39 (pic e).

Continue with the decrease to shape and finish the head as per the Body with Legs instructions.

Make up

Hide any loose wool ends at the top and bottom of the body. See 'hiding wool inside of body' page 116 for instructions.

Lay the ears flat, place under a lightly dampened clean tea towel and press with an iron set on the wool setting. If your iron doesn't have a wool setting, set the heat dial to three-quarters of maximum.

Using mattress stitch (see page 114), take the main colour and sew up the side and the top. Ensure the end of the contrast colour is inside the ear so it stays hidden once the ears are made up.

Sew both ears evenly to the top of the head (see 'sewing onto your work' page 116).

Attach the pompom tail to the base of the body at the back where the legs meet (see 'sewing on pompoms and tassels' page 117) (pic f).

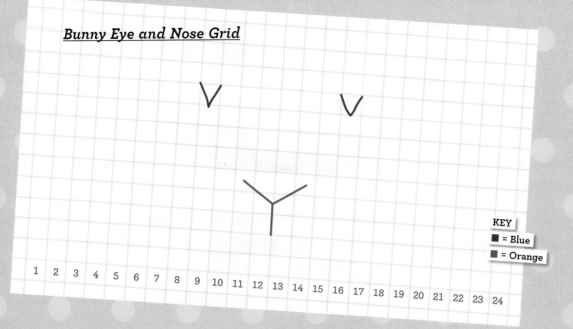

Bunny Eye and Nose Grid

KEY
■ = Blue
■ = Orange

1 2 3 4 5 6 7 8 9 10 11 12 13 14 15 16 17 18 19 20 21 22 23 24

When changing colours to knit the ears, the main and contrasting colours lay side-by-side, looping around each other (b, c). Embroider on the eyes and nose before stuffing and closing the bunny's head (d, e).

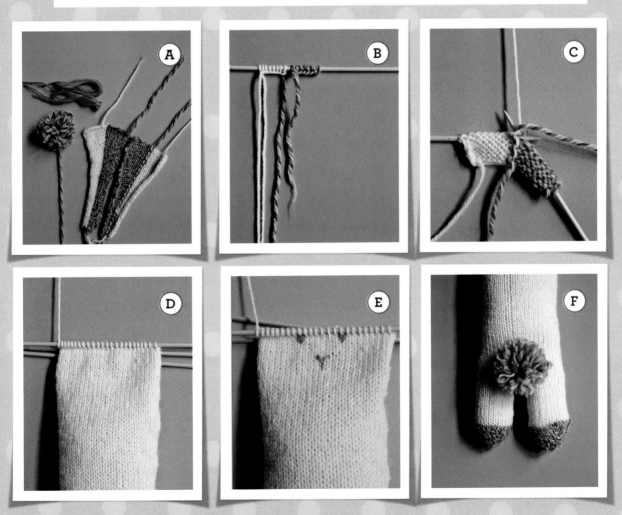

LAZY KOALA

Sleeping, eating, looking cute, "Stress you say?
I don't compute!" If you'd like him 'round for tea
You'll need a eucalyptus tree.

Materials needed

4 x double-pointed 4mm needles
Wool (100g grey for main colour; 50g black for
one foot, the nose and eyes; 50g white for one
foot, the tummy and ears)
Scissors
Stitch holder
Wool needle
Pompom maker
Stuffing

Skills needed

Casting on
Casting off
Knit stitch (K)
Knitting in the round
Increasing stitches (Inc 1)
Decreasing stitches (K2 tog, s1k1 psso)
Changing colours
Transferring stitches to and from a stitch holder
Pompom making
Sewing

*If you are unfamiliar with any of these materials
or skills, turn to pages 6 and 112 for details.*

Tip

The arms have been left off the koala to
keep the pattern simple. If you'd like to
add arms to the koala, follow the 'arms'
instructions for the Gingerbread Man
(page 74) using black wool for the
contrasting colour and grey wool as the
main colour.

Ears

Using a pompom maker with a 60-70mm diameter (centre hole will be around 10mm) and the white wool, make 2 white pompoms. Refer to instructions '*making a pompom*' on page 114.

Tummy

The tummy is knitted flat, using knit stitch for each row to create a garter stitch. You only need 2 x 4mm needles.

Cast on 6 sts with the white wool.

*K1 row.

Begin increase

2nd row: K1, inc 1, k to last 2 sts, inc 1, k1**, (8 sts).

Repeat * to ** until there are 12 sts.

Knit these 12 sts for 18 rows.

Begin decrease

25th row: *K1 row.

26th row: K1, s1k1 psso, k to last 3 sts, k2 tog, k1**, (10 sts).

Repeat * to ** until there are 6 sts.

Cast off.

Cut the wool leaving at least 24cm so you have enough to sew the tummy onto the body. Hide the cast on wool end away as per the '*weaving method*' instructions on page 116.

Nose

The nose is also knitted flat, using knit stitch for each row to create a garter stitch. You only need 2 x 4mm needles.

Cast on 4 sts with the black wool.

K1 row.

Begin increase

2nd row: K1, inc 1, k to last 2 sts, inc 1, k1**, (6 sts).

Repeat * to ** until there are 8 sts.

Work these 8 sts for 3 rows.

Begin decrease

8th row: *K1 row.

9th row: K1, s1k1 psso, k to last 3 sts, k2 tog, k1**, (6 sts).

Repeat * to ** until there are 2 stitches remaining.

Cast off.

Cut the wool leaving at least 16cm so you have enough to sew the nose onto the body. Hide the cast on wool end away as per the '*weaving method*' instructions on page 116.

Body

Follow the instructions for the Body with Legs pattern on page 32, with the following modifications:

Knit 1 foot with a white tip and 1 foot with a black tip (pic b).

Stop when you have completed the 64th body rnd. Make sure that you haven't stuffed right to the top as you will need room for sewing.

Sew on the eyes, using duplicate stitch (see '*embroidery stitches*' page 114), following the grid on page 43.

Continue with the decrease to shape and finish the head as per the Body with Legs instructions.

Ensure the body is stuffed to how firm or soft you want it before you close it up. See page 8 for tips on stuffing.

Make up

Hide any loose wool ends at the top and bottom of the body (see '*hiding wool inside of body*' page 116 for instructions).

Attach the pompom ears securely to the top of the head (see '*sewing on pompoms and tassels*' page 117).

Sew on the tummy and nose (see '*sewing onto your work*' page 116) (pic c).

It's best to sew the tummy and nose on the body after it is stuffed, as stuffing may stretch the stitches a bit if they're sewn on before. The feet were deliberately knitted using mismatched wool (b) – if you prefer, the feet can be the same colour, or use a really bright colour to add a bit of dazzle.

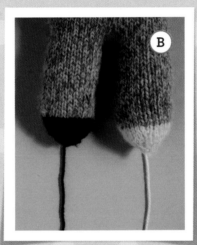

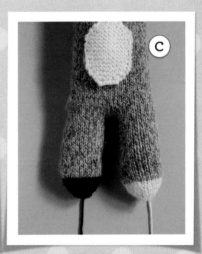

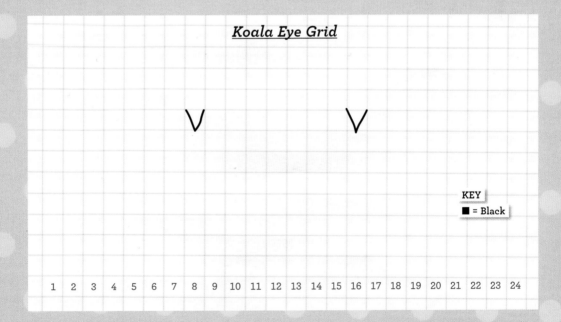

Koala Eye Grid

KEY
■ = Black

CRESTED COCKATOO

Oh cockatoo, well hello you! I heard you're
turning 62! We'll have a cake this afternoon,
I'll bring the candles, you the tune.

Materials needed

4 x double-pointed 4mm needles
Wool (100g white for main colour; 50g dark grey
for legs, beak and eyes; two skeins yellow for the
pompom crest pieces)
Scissors
Stitch holder
Wool needle
Pompom maker
Stuffing

Tip

The cockatoo's crest is made using two
standard-sized pompom makers, but you can
make a larger pompom for a larger crest (trim
it into a punk cut, for a 'cockatoo with attitude'
look). Cockatoos come in many different colours,
so play around with your favourite colours to
create something really special.

Skills needed

Casting on
Casting off
Knit stitch (K)
Knitting in the round
Increasing stitches (Inc 1)
Decreasing stitches (K2 tog, s1k1 psso)
Changing colours
Transferring stitches to and from a stitch holder
Pompom making
Sewing

*If you are unfamiliar with any of these materials
or skills, turn to pages 6 and 112 for details.*

Crest

Using a pompom maker with a 60-70mm diameter (centre hole will be around 10mm) and the yellow wool, make 2 yellow pompoms. Refer to instructions '*making a pompom*' on page 114.

Wings

The wings are knitted flat, using knit stitch for each row to create a garter stitch. You only need 2 x 4mm needles.

Cast on 8 sts with the white wool. Make sure you leave at least 12cm wool hanging so that you have enough to sew the wings onto the body.

K1 row.

2rd row: K1, inc 1, k to last 2 sts, inc 1, k1, (10 sts).

Knit these 10 sts for 23 rows.

Begin decrease

*K1 row.

27th row: S1k1 psso, k to last 2 sts, k2 tog** (8 sts).

Repeat * to ** until there are 2 stitches remaining.

36th row: Pass 1 stitch over the other.

Cut the wool, leaving around 10cm. Thread the loose end through a wool needle then bring it through the remaining stitch. Hide this end away as per the '*weaving method*' instructions on page 116.

Repeat for the 2nd wing.

Beak

The beak is also knitted flat, using knit stitch for each row to create a garter stitch. You only need 2 x 4mm needles.

Cast on 8 sts with the dark grey wool.

*K1 row.

Begin decrease

2nd row: S1k1 psso, k to last 2 sts, k2 tog**, (6 sts).

Repeat * to ** until 2 stitches remain.

Cut the wool leaving at least 16cm so you have enough to sew the beak onto the body.

Hide the cast on end away as per the '*weaving method*' instructions on page 116.

Body

Follow the instructions for the Body with Legs pattern on page 32, with the following modifications:

Knit the legs with the dark grey wool, switching to the M colour, white, where the legs join to form the body (pic b).

Stop when you have completed the 64th body rnd. Make sure you haven't stuffed right to the top as you will need room for sewing.

Sew on the eyes, using duplicate stitch (see '*embroidery stitches*' page 114), following the grid on page 47.

Continue with the decrease to shape and finish the head as per the Body with Legs instructions.

Ensure the body is stuffed to how firm or soft you want it before you close it up. See page 8 for tips on stuffing.

Make up

Hide any loose wool ends at the top and bottom of the body (see '*hiding wool inside of body*' page 116 for instructions).

Attach the pompom crest pieces, one behind the other, at the top of the head. As a guideline, ensure the bases are around 15mm apart so that they are close together and create a nice full crest. See '*sewing on pompoms and tassels*' page 117.

Sew the beak on between the eyes, and the wings on the sides of the body as pictured on page 45 (see '*sewing onto your work*' page 116).

It's best to sew the beak and wings onto the body after it is stuffed, as the stuffing may stretch the stitches a bit if they're sewn on before. This pattern differs slightly from the main Body with Legs pattern, in that the legs are knitted in a different colour to the body, and there is no contrasting colour for the feet (b).

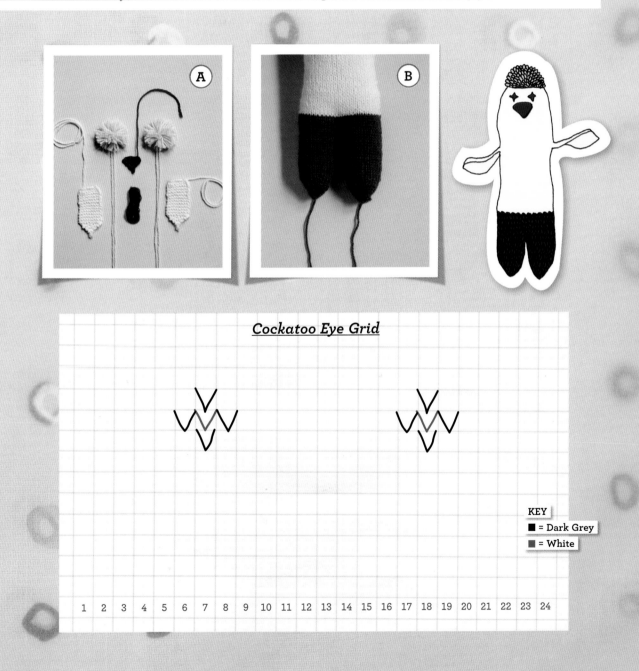

Cockatoo Eye Grid

KEY
■ = Dark Grey
■ = White

1 2 3 4 5 6 7 8 9 10 11 12 13 14 15 16 17 18 19 20 21 22 23 24

ZIPPY ZEBRA

Running in the Serengeti, Zebra's stride
is firm and steady, If a lion is about
Her camouflage will help her out.

Materials needed

4 x double-pointed 4mm needles
Wool (100g white, 100g black, one small skein of pink for nostrils)
Scissors
Stitch holder
Wool needle
Pompom maker
50mm tassel square
Stuffing

Skills needed

Casting on
Casting off
Knit stitch (K)
Knitting in the round
Increasing stitches (Inc 1)
Decreasing stitches (K2 tog, s1k1 psso)
Changing colours
Pompom making
Tassel making
Transferring stitches to and from a stitch holder
Sewing

If you are unfamiliar with any of these materials or skills, turn to pages 6 and 112 for details.

Nose

The nose is knitted flat, using knit stitch for each row to create a garter stitch. You only need 2 x 4mm needles.

Cast on 4 sts with the black wool. Make sure you leave at least 12cm wool hanging so you have enough to sew the nose onto the face.

Knit 1 row.

Begin increase

2nd row: K1, inc 1, inc 1, k1, (6 sts).

Knit 1 row.

4th row: K1, inc 1, k2, inc 1, k1, (8 sts).

Knit 3 rows.

Begin decrease

8th row: K1, s1k1 psso, k2, k2 tog, k1, (6 sts).

Knit 1 row.

10th row: K1, s1k1 psso, k2 tog, k1, (4 sts).

Cast off. Hide the wool end away as per the *'weaving method'* instructions on page 116.

Sew the nostrils onto the nose using duplicate stitch (see *'embroidery stitches'* page 114) and the pink wool, following the grid on page 51.

Ears

The ears are also knitted flat, using knit stitch for each row to create a garter stitch. You only need 2 x 4mm needles.

Cast on 8 sts with the white wool. Ensure you leave at least 12cm wool hanging to finish the ears and sew them onto the zebra's head.

*Knit 1 row.

2nd row: S1k1 psso, k to last 2 sts, k2 tog** (6 sts)

Repeat * to ** until 2 stitches remain.

Knit 1 row.

8th row: Pass 1 st over the other, (1 st).

Cut the wool, leaving around 10cm. Thread a wool needle and pull the loose end through the remaining stitch and hide this end away as per the 'weaving method' instructions on page 116.

Pinch the ear to make it more pointed and angled.

Lay the ear flat, thread a wool needle with the leftover wool from the cast on and use this to sew the two bottom corners together. Pull this tightly and then remove the needle and put aside. When you attach the ears to the body use this wool end. (Refer to Wobbly Wombat pics b, c page 17).

Repeat steps to make the 2nd ear.

Mane

Using a pompom maker with a 40-50mm diameter (centre hole will be around 10mm) and the black wool make 4 pompoms. Refer to instructions 'making a pompom' on page 114.

Tail

Using the black wool, make one tassel around 50mm in length, following the tassel instructions on page 114.

Body

Follow the instructions for the Body with Legs pattern on page 32 with the following modification to create the stripes – alternate the black and white wools as per the following instructions:

Legs

Cast on and work the increase with the black wool. Follow the 24 rnds for the leg to the following pattern:

Work 8 rnds white.

Work 8 rnds black.

Work 8 rnds white.

Body

Join legs together and begin with 8 rnds black.

Switch between white and black every 8 rnds.

Stop when you have completed the 64th body rnd. Make sure you haven't stuffed right to the top as you will need room for sewing.

Sew on the eyes using duplicate stitch (see 'embroidery stitches' page 114) following the grid on page 51.

Continue with the decrease to shape and finish the head with black wool as per the Body with Legs instructions.

When switching wools, it may be easier to leave the wool attached and carry it up when you begin the next stripe. Ensure you don't pull the wool end too tightly when you carry it up to switch colours, there should be a little bit of slack (pics b, c).

Ensure the body is stuffed to how firm or soft you want it before you close it up. See page 8 for tips on stuffing.

Make up

Hide any loose wool ends at the top and bottom of the body (see 'hiding wool inside of body' page 116 for instructions).

Sew on the 5 black pompoms for the mane, beginning at the top of the head and spacing them around 10-15mm apart (see 'sewing on pompoms and tassels' page 117).

Sew the ears onto either side of the mane (see 'sewing onto your work' page 116). Make sure the ears are standing erect – zebras use their ears to show their mood, and ears standing at attention can mean they are feeling calm or friendly.

Sew on the nose (see 'sewing onto your work' page 116).

Attach the tassel tail to the base of the body at the back where the legs meet (see 'sewing on pompoms and tassels' page 117).

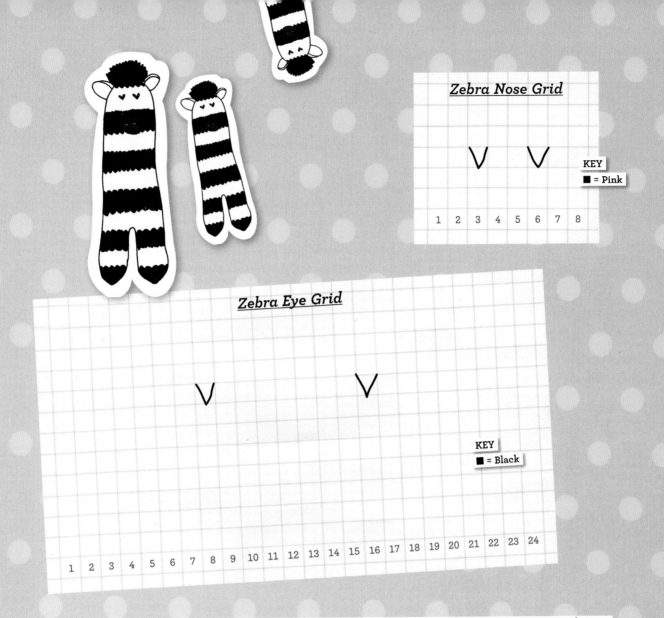

Zebra Nose Grid

V   V

KEY
■ = Pink

1 2 3 4 5 6 7 8

Zebra Eye Grid

V   V

KEY
■ = Black

1 2 3 4 5 6 7 8 9 10 11 12 13 14 15 16 17 18 19 20 21 22 23 24

It's easier to leave the wool attached and to simply carry it up when you are switching colours between stripes (c). It's best to sew the nose, tail and mane onto the body after it is stuffed, as stuffing may stretch the stitches if they're sewn on before.

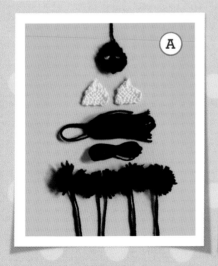

SCAREDY LION

Lion has a mighty roar, It lifts the dust right off the floor! He may be king, but can't contend, With the spines of his echidna friend, So when you have them 'round to eat, Be sure they're not on adjacent seats.

Materials needed

4 x double-pointed 4mm needles
Wool (100g yellow for body and mane; 50g light brown for face; 50g orange for 1 foot and mane; 50g medium brown for 1 foot, mane and nose; skeins of black and blue for the eyes and whiskers)
Scissors
Stitch holder
Wool needle
Pompom maker
Stuffing
French knitting tool
Crochet hook (optional but recommended)

Skills needed

Casting on
Knit stitch (K)
Knitting in the round
Increasing stitches (Inc 1)
Decreasing stitches (K2 tog, s1k1 psso)
Changing colours
Pompom making
Duplicate stitch embroidery
Transferring stitches to and from a stitch holder
French knitting

If you are unfamiliar with any of these materials or skills, turn to pages 6 and 112 for details.

Nose

The nose is knitted flat, using knit stitch for each row to create a garter stitch. You only need 2 x 4mm needles.

Cast on 5 sts with the medium brown wool, leaving at least 10cm wool hanging so you have enough to sew the nose onto the face.

Knit 2 rows.

Begin decrease

3rd row: S1k1 psso, k1, k2 tog. (3 sts).

Knit 2 rows.

6th row: Pass 1 st over the other, (2 sts).

Cast off. Hide the wool end away as per the *'weaving method'* instructions on page 116.

Mane

We made 11 pompoms to create the lion's mane, combining medium brown, orange and yellow wools (similar to *Nosey Echidna*, pics a, b, c, page 25) and using a pompom maker with a 60-70mm diameter (centre hole will be around 10mm). Refer to instructions '*making a pompom*' on page 114.

Tail

Using the yellow wool and the French knitting technique (see page 115), create a cord that is 50mm in length. Cut the working wool end, leaving around 10cm so that you can sew the tail to the body. Using the wool needle, thread the wool end through the 4 sts as you remove them from the French knitting tool.

Using a pompom maker with a 25mm diameter (centre hole will be around 10mm) and the medium brown wool, make 1 pompom.

Sew the pompom onto one end of the tail (see '*sewing on pompoms and tassels*' page 117).

Body

Follow the instructions for the Body with Legs pattern on page 32, with the following modifications:

Knit 1 foot with an orange tip and 1 foot with a medium brown tip.

Work 40 body rnds with yellow wool.

Switch to light brown wool and work 24 rnds.

Stop after the 64th body rnd. Sew on the eyes using duplicate stitch and the whiskers (pic b) using straight stitch (see '*embroidery stitches*' page 114), following the grid on page 55.

Ensure the body is stuffed to how firm or soft you want it before beginning the ears. See page 8 for tips on stuffing.

Shaping the ears

Take 24 sts (12 from the right front and 12 from the right back needle (pic c) and transfer them to a stitch holder. Reconfigure the 3 needles (6-12-6), with the 12-st needle across the front of your work.

65th rnd: *K4, k2 tog**, repeat *to** for the entire rnd, (5-10-5) 20 sts.

Work 1 rnd.

67th rnd: *K3, k2 tog**, repeat *to** for the entire rnd, (4-8-4) 16 sts.

Work 1 rnd.

69th rnd: *K2, k2 tog**, repeat *to** for the entire rnd, (3-6-3) 12 sts.

Work 1 rnd.

71st rnd: *K1, k2 tog**, repeat *to** for the entire rnd, (2-4-2) 8 sts.

Work 1 rnd.

73rd rnd: K2 tog for the entire rnd, (1-2-1) 4 sts.

Cut the wool leaving around 10cm. Thread a wool needle and pass it through these 4 sts as you pull them off the needle.

Transfer the stitches from the stitch holder and place them across the 3 needles (6-12-6) as per the first ear.

Repeat these steps for the 2nd ear.

Ensure the ears are stuffed to how firm or soft you want them before finishing the second ear.

Make up

Hide any loose wool ends at the top and bottom of the body (see '*hiding wool inside of body*' page 116 for instructions).

Sew the nose on securely (see '*sewing onto your work*' page 116).

Sew the tail to the base of the body at the back where the legs meet.

Attach the pompom mane around the head, using the main picture as a guide. Place one in the centre of the ears and one about 15mm behind it. Place one behind each ear, three down each side of his face and one at the bottom of his face. Space them about 25mm apart (see '*sewing on pompoms and tassels*' page 117).

Sew the small gap between the ears closed (refer to pictures h and i on page 35 – while these pictures show sewing the gap between the legs, it is similar to sewing up between the ears).

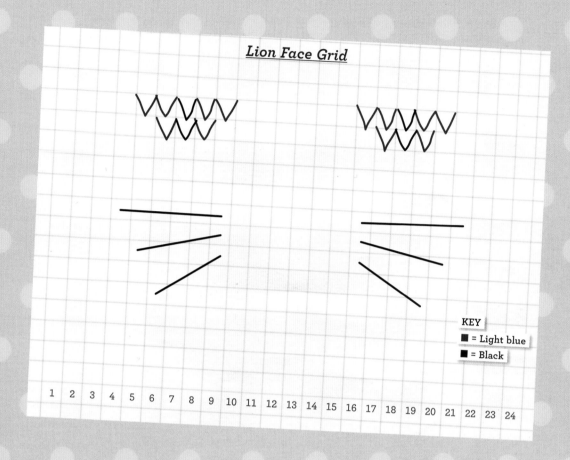

Lion Face Grid

KEY
- ■ = Light blue
- ■ = Black

1 2 3 4 5 6 7 8 9 10 11 12 13 14 15 16 17 18 19 20 21 22 23 24

The pompoms are made using multiple colours (see pictures a and b Nosey Echidna, page 25). Embroider the lion's eyes and whiskers onto the face before shaping the ears (b). Configure the needles when shaping the lion's ears (c).

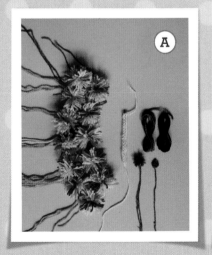

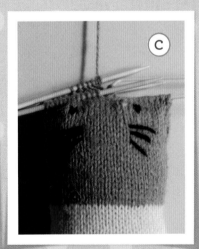

FLYING UNICORN

Her purple horn is made of joy, The unicorn is a magic toy
Flip her tail and click her hoof, Then watch her fly
straight through the roof!

Materials needed

4 x double-pointed 4mm needles
Wool (100g white for body and nose; 50g yellow for feet, hooves, eyes, mane and tail; 50 purple for horn, mane, tail and nostrils; 25g each pink, green and blue for mane and tail)
Scissors
Stitch holder
Wool needle
Pompom maker
50mm tassel square
35mm tassel square
Stuffing

Skills needed

Casting on
Casting off
Knit stitch (K)
Knitting in the round
Increasing stitches (Inc 1)
Decreasing stitches (K2 tog, s1k1 psso)
Changing colours
Transferring stitches to and from a stitch holder
Pompom making
Tassel making
Sewing

If you are unfamiliar with any of these materials or skills, turn to pages 6 and 112 for details.

Nose

The nose is knitted flat, using knit stitch for each row to create a garter stitch. You only need 2 x 4mm needles.

Cast on 4 sts with the white wool. Make sure you leave at least 12cm wool hanging so you have enough to sew the nose onto the face.

Knit 1 row.

Begin increase

2nd row: K1, inc 1, inc 1, k1. (6 sts).

Knit 1 row.

4th row: K1, inc 1, k2, inc 1, k1. (8 sts).

Knit 3 rows.

Begin decrease

8th row: K1, s1k1 psso, k2, k2 tog, k1. (6 sts).

Knit 1 row.

10th row: K1, s1k1 psso, k2 tog, k1. (4 sts).

Cast off. Hide the wool end away as per the *'weaving method'* instructions on page 116.

Take the purple wool, and using duplicate stitch (see *'embroidery stitches'* page 114) sew on the 2 nostrils following the grid on page 59.

Ears

The ears are also knitted flat, using knit stitch for each row to create a garter stitch. You only need 2 x 4mm needles.

Cast on 8 sts with the white wool, leaving at least 12cm wool hanging to finish the ears and attach them to the unicorn's head.

*Knit 1 row.

2nd row: S1k1 psso, k to last 2 sts, k2 tog**, (6 sts)

Repeat * to ** until 2 stitches remain.

Knit 1 row.

8th row: Pass 1 st over the other, (1 st).

Cut the wool, leaving around 10cm. Thread the loose end through a wool needle then bring it through the remaining stitch. Hide this end away as per the '_weaving method_' instructions on page 116.

Pinch the ear together to create a more pointed and angled effect. Refer to _Wobbly Wombat_ 'Ears' page 16, and pics b, c page 17, on how to sew up the ear. Repeat this process to make the 2nd ear.

Horn

The horn is knit entirely in the round using 4 x 4mm double-pointed needles. This is the trickiest part of making the unicorn – to make the point, you end up with only 4 sts on the needles, which can be fiddly. Don't give up, it is only a small bit!

Cast on 10 sts using the purple wool, leaving at least 12cm hanging to sew the horn on the head.

Split the sts across 3 needles (3-6-3).

Work 2 rnds.

3rd rnd: K4, s1k1 psso, k4, (3-3-3) 9 sts.

Work 2 rnds.

6th rnd: K3, s1k1 psso, k4, (3-2-3) 8 sts.

Work 2 rnds.

9th rnd: K3, s1k1 psso, k2, (3-1-3) 7 sts.

Reconfigure your sts to 2-3-2.

Work 2 rnds.

12th rnd: K2, s1k1 psso, k3, 6 sts (2-2-2).

Work 2 rnds.

15th rnd: K2, s1k1 psso, k2, (2-1-2) 5 sts.

Work 2 rnds.

18th rnd: S1k1 psso, k3, (4 sts).

Word 2 rnds.

Cut the wool, leaving 12cm hanging. Thread a wool needle and pull the wool through the 4 sts, removing them from the needle as you go.

Rainbow tail

Using the pink, yellow, green, blue and purple wools make 1 tassel (see page 114) around 50mm in length. To create the rainbow effect, wrap each wool around the tassel board 5 times (pic b). Use pink to tie it off, and hide the ends with the pink part of the tail.

Rainbow mane

The mane is made with 5 different coloured tassels – pink, yellow, green, blue and purple (see page 114). We used a 35mm tassel board to make ours but you can make the mane as long as you want. We recommend 60mm as a maximum length.

Body

Follow the instructions for the Body with Legs pattern on page 32, with the following modifications:

Stop when you have completed the 64th body rnd. Make sure you don't stuff right to the top as you need room for sewing.

Sew on the eyes using duplicate stitch (see '_embroidery stitches_' page 114), following the grid on page 59.

Continue with the decrease to shape and finish the head as per the Body with Legs instructions.

Make up

Hide any loose wool ends at the top and bottom of the body (see '_hiding wool inside of body_' page 116 for instructions).

For the mane, sew the coloured tassels 15mm apart, starting at the top of unicorn's head and going down slightly off to one side (see '_sewing on pompoms and tassels_' page 117).

Sew the nose on securely (see '_sewing onto your work_' page 116). Sew on the ears and horn (pic c).

Attach the tassel tail to the base of the body at the back where the legs meet (see '_sewing on pompoms and tassels_' page 117).

Unicorn Nose Grid

V V

KEY
■ = Purple

1 2 3 4 5 6 7 8

Unicorn Eye Grid

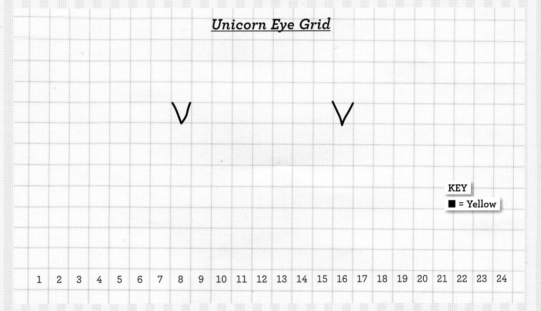

V V

KEY
■ = Yellow

1 2 3 4 5 6 7 8 9 10 11 12 13 14 15 16 17 18 19 20 21 22 23 24

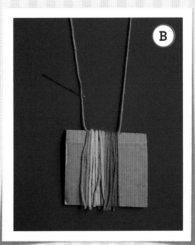

COOL CAT

His personal care is second to none, He licks his paws
and fur – for fun! Dazzle him with string and fluff?
He's way too cool for all that stuff.

Materials needed

6 x double-pointed 4mm needles
Wool (100g burgundy for main colour; 25g light
brown for tail tip; 25g hot pink for ears; skeins of
black, turquoise and orange for eyes, nose and
whiskers)
Scissors
Stitch holder
Wool needle
Stuffing

Skills needed

Casting on
Casting off
Knit stitch (K)
Knitting in the round
Increasing stitches (Inc 1)
Decreasing stitches (K2 tog, s1k1 psso)
Changing colours
Transferring stitches to and from a stitch holder
3-needle joining

*If you are unfamiliar with any of these materials
or skills, turn to pages 6 and 112 for details.*

Nose

The nose is knitted flat, using knit stitch for
each row to create a garter stitch. You only
need 2 x 4mm needles.

Cast on 5 sts with the orange wool. Make sure
you leave at least 10cm wool hanging so you
have enough to sew the nose onto the face.

Knit 2 rows.

Begin decrease

3rd row: S1k1 psso, k1, k2 tog, (3 sts).

Knit 2 rows.

6th row: Pass 1 st over the other, (2 sts).

Cast off. Hide the wool end away as per the
'weaving method' instructions on page 116.

Tail

The tail is made exactly as per a leg in the Body with Legs pattern (see page 32), except work for 40 rnds instead of 24.

We used light brown as the contrast colour for the end of the tail.

Close off the tail so there is one row of stitches – this will allow the tail to be knit directly onto the body. This is done using a 3-needle joining method (see page 114 for instructions). Be sure not to bind off as you go, just knit the 2 stitches together to create 1 stitch on the opposite needle (pics b, c).

Leave these stitches on the needle – they are used to join the tail to the body (pic d).

Body

Follow the instructions for the Body with Legs pattern on page 32, with the following modifications:

We haven't used any contrast colour for cat's feet – we have used main (M) all the way up. You can use the light brown wool, or any colour you like, for a contrast (C) colour.

Stop once you have completed 7 body rnds. The tail is now joined using the 3-needle joining method (see page 114).

8th rnd: Work 8th rnd, but stop 6 stitches out from the centre (i.e., where the legs meet); take the needle with the tail and lie this parallel to the working needle (aligning the 12 tail stitches with the 12 centre stitches) next to where the tail will join the body.

With the needles parallel, knit through 2 stitches at once, creating 1 stitch (see '3-needle joining' pages 114-115). As you continue to knit the tail will be joined securely to the body (pic e).

Continue to knit the rest of the body as per the Body with Legs instructions.

Stop when you have completed the 64th body rnd. Make sure you haven't stuffed right to the top as you will need room for sewing.

Sew on the eyes using duplicate stitch and the whiskers using straight stitches (see 'embroidery stitches' page 114), following the grid on page 63.

Ensure the body is stuffed to how firm or soft you want it before beginning the ears. See page 8 for tips on stuffing.

Shaping the ears

Take 24 stitches (12 from the right front and 12 from the right back (see pic c, *Scaredy Lion*, page 55) and place them on a stitch holder. Reconfigure the 3 needles (6-12-6), with the 12-stitch needle across the front, as pictured.

Join the hot pink wool (see '*joining new wool or changing colours*' page 116).

65th rnd: *K4, k2 tog**, repeat *to** for the entire rnd, (5-10-5) 20 sts.

Work 1 rnd.

67th rnd: *K3, k2 tog**, repeat *to** for the entire rnd, (4-8-4) 16 sts.

Work 1 rnd.

69th rnd: *K2, k2 tog**, repeat *to** for the entire rnd, (3-6-3) 12 sts.

Work 1 rnd.

71st rnd: *K1, k2 tog**, repeat *to** for the entire rnd, (2-4-2) 8 sts.

Work 1 rnd.

73rd rnd: K2 tog for the entire rnd, (1-2-1) 4 sts.

Cut the wool leaving around 10cm. Thread a wool needle and pass it through these 4 sts as you pull them off the needle.

Transfer the stitches from the stitch holder onto 3 needles (6-12-6) as per the first ear. Repeat these steps for the 2nd ear.

Ensure the ears are stuffed to how firm or soft you want them before finishing the second ear (pic f).

Make up

Hide any loose wool ends at the top and bottom of the body (see '*hiding wool inside of body*' page 116).

Sew the nose on securely (see '*sewing onto your work*' page 116).

Sew the small gap between the ears closed (refer to pictures h and i on page 35 – while these pictures show sewing the gap between the legs, it is similar to sewing up between the ears).

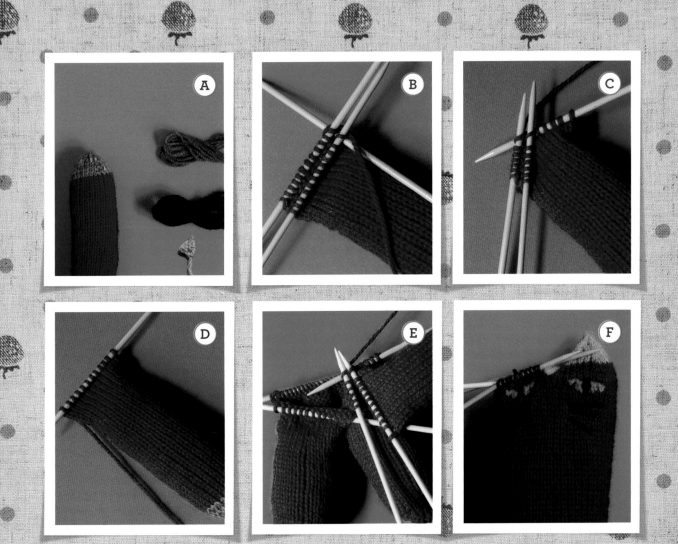

Cat Face Grid

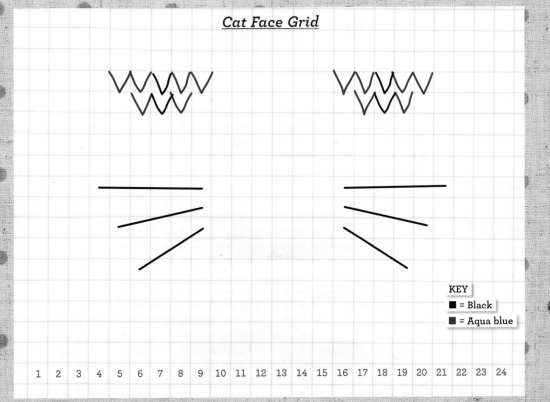

KEY
■ = Black
■ = Aqua blue

| 1 | 2 | 3 | 4 | 5 | 6 | 7 | 8 | 9 | 10 | 11 | 12 | 13 | 14 | 15 | 16 | 17 | 18 | 19 | 20 | 21 | 22 | 23 | 24 |

SUPER SLOTH

When they were assigning super powers, Some could fly
or scale high towers, The sloth's attraction is all tempo
His super power is being slow.

Materials needed

8 x double-pointed 4mm needles
Wool (100g medium brown tweed wool; 50g dark
brown for paws, nose and eye detail; 25g white
for face; skein of black for smile and eyes)
Scissors
Stitch holder
Wool needle
Stuffing

Skills needed

Casting on
Casting off
Knit stitch (K)
Purl stitch (P)
Knitting in the round
Increasing stitches (Inc 1)
Decreasing stitches (K2 tog, s1k1 psso)
Changing colours
Transferring stitches to and from a stitch holder
3-needle joining
Sewing

*If you are unfamiliar with any of these materials
or skills, turn to pages 6 and 112 for details.*

Arms

The arms are made exactly as per a leg in the
Body with Legs pattern (see page 32), except
work for 48 rnds instead of 24.

We used dark brown as our contrast (C) colour
for the end of the arms.

Ensure the arm is stuffed, leaving around 25mm
unstuffed at the top where the needles are.

Close off the arms so there is 1 row of stitches;
this will allow the arms to be knit directly onto
the body.

This is done using a 3-needle joining method (see
page 114 for instructions). Be sure not to bind off
as you go, just knit the 2 stitches together to
create 1 stitch on the opposite needle.

Leave these stitches on the needle; they are used
to join the arms to the body (pic a).

Face

The face is knitted flat, using knit and purl
stitches on alternating rows to create stocking
stitch. You only need 2 x 4mm needles.

Cast on 6 sts with the white wool, leaving at
least 20cm wool hanging so you have enough
to sew the face onto the body.

1st row: P

Begin increase

2nd row: K1, inc 1, k2, inc 1, k1, (8 sts).

3rd row: P

4th row: K1, inc 1, k4, inc 1, k1, (10 sts).

5th row: P

6th row: K1, inc 1, k6, inc 1, k1, (12 sts).

7th row: P

8th row: K1, inc 1, k8, inc 1, k1, (14 sts).

9th row: P

10th row: K1, inc 1, k10, inc 1, k1, (16 sts).

Work 5 rows stocking st, finishing after a P

Begin decrease

16th row: K1, s1k1 psso, k10, k2 tog, k1, (14 sts).

17th row: P

18th row: K1, s1k1 psso, k8, k2 tog, k1, (12 sts).

19th row: P

20th row: K1, s1k1 psso, k6, k2 tog, k1, (10 sts).

21st row: P

22nd row: K1, s1k1 psso, k4, k2 tog, k1, (8 sts).

23rd row: P

24th: K1, s1k1 psso, k2, k2 tog, k1, (6 sts).

25th row: P

Cast off.

Sew on the eyes and nose using duplicate stitch and the smile using a large, loose straight stitch with couching stitches (see '*embroidery stitches*' page 114), following the grid on page 67 (pic b).

Body

Follow the instructions for the Body with Legs pattern on page 32, with the following modifications:

Stop once you have completed 39 body rnds.

The arms are now joined using the 3-needle joining method (see page 114).

The arms should be centred on either side of the body, so align the arm stitches with 6 stitches from the front and 6 stitches from the back.

40th rnd: Work 40th rnd, but stop 6 sts from the end of the front needle; take the needle with the arm and lie this parallel to the working needle (aligning the 12 arm stitches with the 6 front stitches next to where the arm will join the body (pics c, d, e).

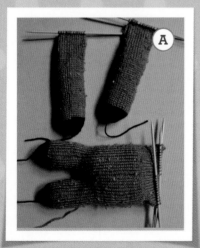

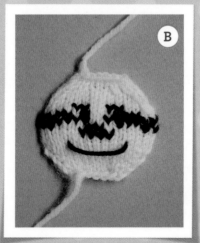

With the needles parallel, knit through 2 stitches at once, creating 1 stitch (see *3-needle joining* pages 114-115). Once you have completed the 6 stitches on the front, wrap the arm around to the back and repeat the process for the back stitches.

Complete this process for the 2nd arm.

Continue as per the Body with Legs instructions.

Ensure the body is stuffed to how firm or soft you want it before you close it up. See page 8 for tips on stuffing.

Make up

Hide any loose wool ends at the top and bottom of the body (see '*hiding wool inside of body*' page 116).

Lay the face flat under a lightly dampened clean tea towel; press with an iron set to wool setting (or set to three-quarters of maximum).

Sew the face on securely (see '*sewing onto your work*' page 116).

Create his signature three yellow toes by making three straight stitches (see '*embroidery stitches*' page 114) across each paw (see pic f, and main picture page 65).

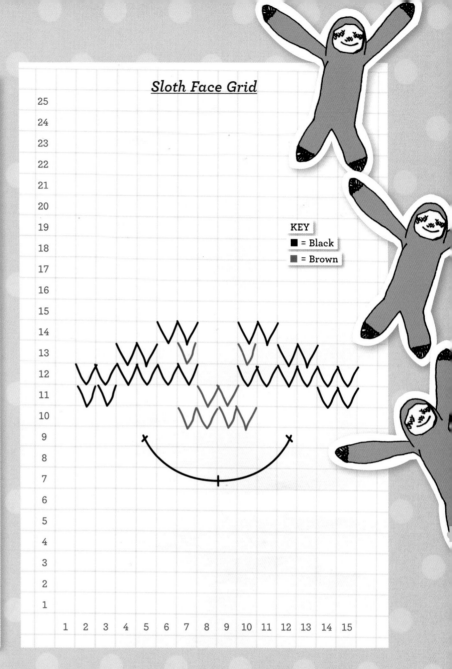

Sloth Face Grid

KEY
■ = Black
■ = Brown

D

E

F

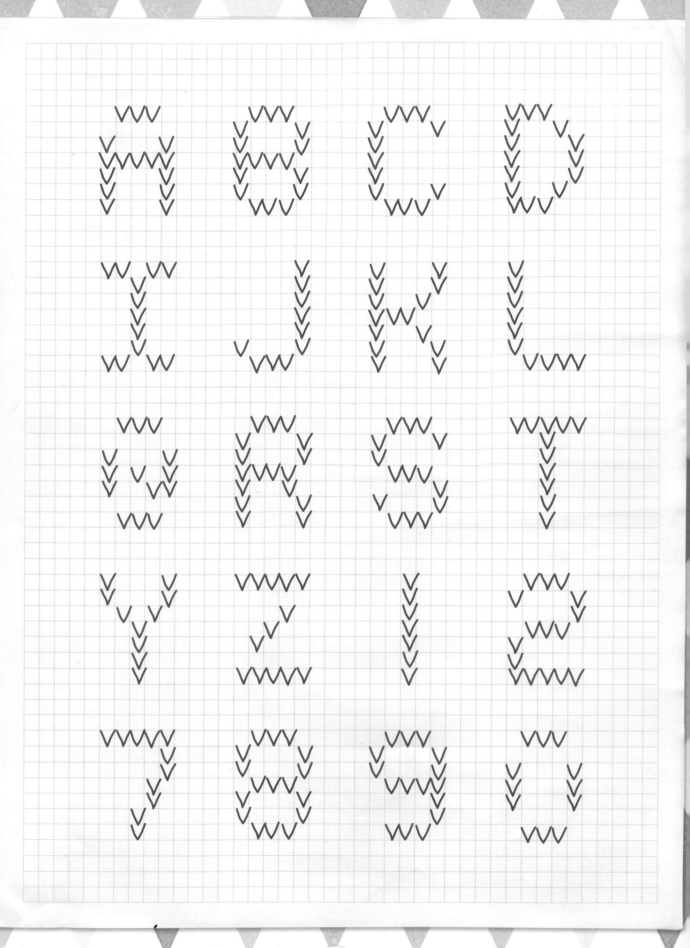

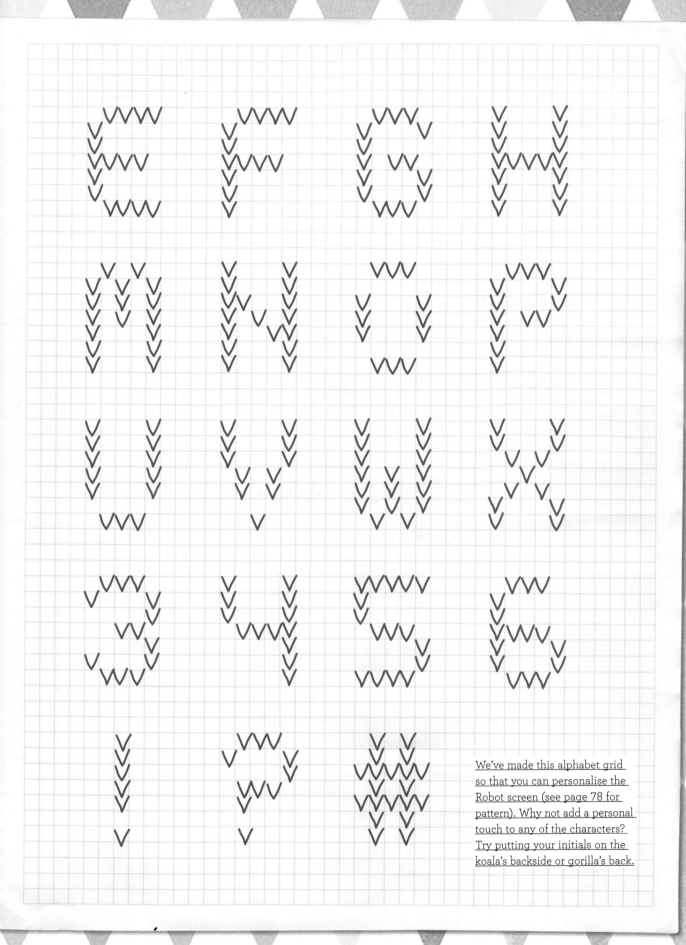

We've made this alphabet grid so that you can personalise the Robot screen (see page 78 for pattern). Why not add a personal touch to any of the characters? Try putting your initials on the koala's backside or gorilla's back.

RAINBOW ELEPHANT

His trunk is a nose with many great powers, It can smell, it can sing –
it can even give showers! He's a colourful creature – you want to
know why? He was dipped in a rainbow that fell from the sky.

Materials needed

6 x double-pointed 4mm needles
Wool (50g light grey for body; 50g pink for legs,
face and pompom ears; 25g yellow for foot and
pompom ears; 25g blue for foot and pompom
ears; skeins of black and red for trunk and eye
embroidery)
Scissors
Stitch holder
Wool needle
Pompom maker
Stuffing

◇◇◇◇◇◇◇◇◇◇◇◇◇◇◇◇◇◇◇◇◇◇◇◇

Skills needed

Casting on
Casting off
Knit stitch (K)
Knitting in the round
Increasing stitches (Inc 1)
Decreasing stitches (K2 tog, s1k1 psso)
Changing colours
Pompom making
3-needle joining
Sewing

*If you are unfamiliar with any of these materials
or skills, turn to pages 6 and 112 for details.*

◇◇◇◇◇◇◇◇◇◇◇◇◇◇◇◇◇◇◇◇◇◇◇◇

Tip

We've played around with the colours to
make the elephant a bit different – he was
actually inspired by the Jungle Elephant
in the Australian Women's Weekly best-
selling *'The Children's Birthday Cake Book'.*
The elephant doesn't need to be quite so
rainbow coloured – try combining different
shades of grey for a more traditionally
coloured elephant, or shades of your
favourite colour for something special.
If you'd like the elephant to have upper
limbs, follow the 'arms' instructions for the
Gingerbread Man (page 74) using your
colours of choice.

Trunk

The trunk is made exactly as a leg (see page 32). Ensure you leave around 12cm wool hanging after casting on to tie up the end of the trunk.

There is no contrast (C) colour at the tip of the trunk and it is not stuffed, instead the end of the trunk is folded and pointed (some people say it is bad luck to have his trunk pointing down!). Fold up the end of the trunk and, using the wool left after casting on, simply sew the tip onto the trunk (pics b, c).

Sew on the trunk detail using 3 straight stitches (see 'embroidery stitches' page 114) and the main picture (page 71) as a guide.

Close off the trunk so there is 1 row of stitches - this allows the trunk to be knitted directly onto the body.

To do this, use the 3-needle joining method (see page 114 for instructions).

Ears

Using a pompom maker with a 70-80mm diameter (centre hole will be around 10mm), make 2 pompoms using the blue, pink and yellow wool (similar to *Nosey Echidna*, pics a and b page 25). Refer to '*making a pompom*' instructions on page 114.

Body

Follow the instructions for the Body with Legs pattern on page 32, with the following modifications:

Switch to light grey wool when you join the legs to form the body (see '*joining new wool or changing colours*' page 116) (pic d).

Switch to pink wool after 40 body rnds.

Stop after 47 body rnds. Join the trunk using the 3-needle joining method (page 114).

Centre the trunk on the front of the body (pics e, f). On the needle with 12 stitches, knit 6. Take the needle with the trunk aligning the 12 trunk stitches to where you would like to join the trunk to the body.

With the needles parallel, knit through 2 stitches at once, creating 1 stitch (see *3-needle joining* pages 114-115). As you continue to knit, the trunk will be joined securely to the body.

Stop when you have completed the 64th body rnd. Make sure you haven't stuffed right to the top as you will need room for sewing.

Sew on the eyes using duplicate stitch and the eyelashes using straight stitches (see '*embroidery stitches*' page 114) following the grid on page 73.

Continue with the decrease to shape and finish the head as per the Body with Legs instructions.

Ensure the body is stuffed to how firm or soft you want it before you close it up. See page 8 for tips on stuffing.

Make up

Hide any loose wool ends at the feet, head and trunk (see '*hiding wool inside of body*' page 116).

Attach the pompom ears securely to the body (see '*sewing on pompoms and tassels*' page 117).

Elephant Eye Grid

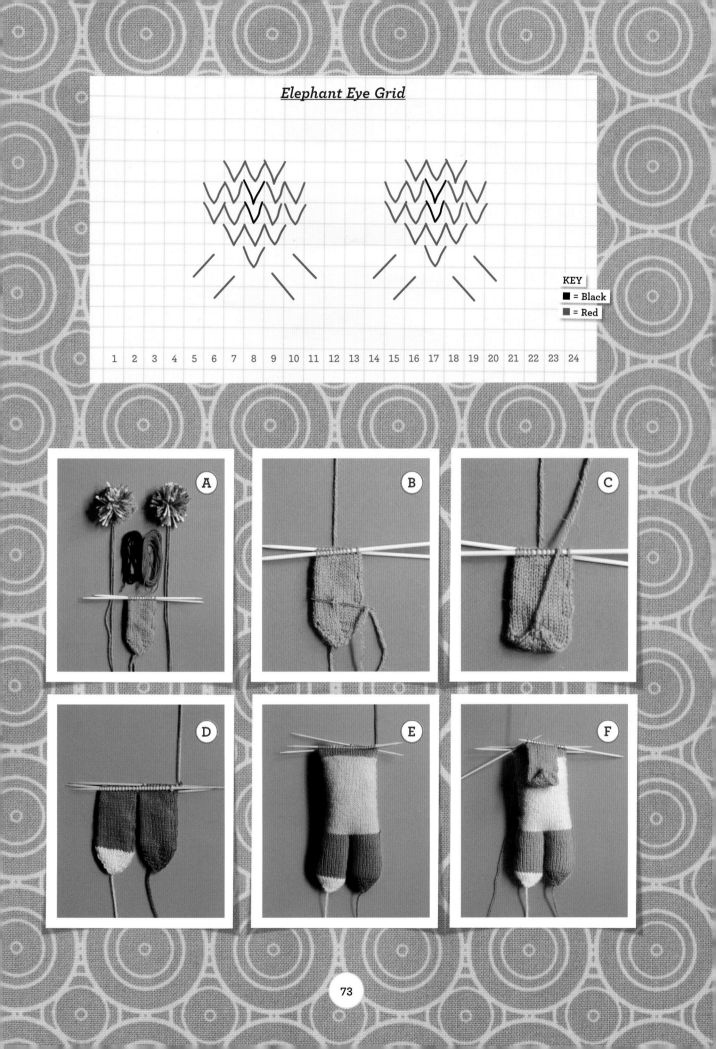

KEY
■ = Black
■ = Red

1 2 3 4 5 6 7 8 9 10 11 12 13 14 15 16 17 18 19 20 21 22 23 24

GINGERBREAD MAN

Our hero from a baking fable, A favourite on the
Christmas table, It's easy looking fine and dandy,
When your wardrobe's made of candy!

Materials needed

8 x double-pointed 4mm needles
Wool (100g light brown for main colour;
50g white for feet and hands, eyes and buttons;
skeins of yellow, green, red and black for eyes,
nose, buttons and mouth.)
Scissors
Stitch holder
Wool needle
Stuffing

Skills needed

Casting on
Casting off
Knit stitch (K)
Knitting in the round
Increasing stitches (Inc 1)
Decreasing stitches (K2 tog, s1k1 psso)
Changing colours
Transferring stitches to and from a stitch holder
3-needle joining

If you are unfamiliar with any of these materials
or skills, turn to pages 6 and 112 for details.

Arms

The arms are made exactly as per a leg
(see Body with Legs, page 32).

We used white as our contrast (C) colour for
the end of the arms.

Close off the arms so there is 1 row of stitches –
this allows the arms to be knitted directly onto
the body.

Use the 3-needle joining method, see page 114
for instructions.

Body

Follow the instructions for Body with Legs pattern
on page 32, with the following modifications:

Stop once you have completed 39 body rnds.
Make sure you haven't stuffed right to the top
as you will need room for sewing.

Sew on the buttons using duplicate stitch (see
'embroidery stitches' page 114) following the grid
on page 75 (pics b, c).

Join the arms using the 3-needle joining method
(see pages 114–115).

The arms should be centred either side of the
body, so align the arm stitches with 6 stitches
from the front and 6 stitches from the back.

40th rnd: Work 40th rnd, but stop 6 sts from the end of the front needle; take the needle with the first arm and lie this parallel to the working needle (aligning the 12 arm stitches with the 6 front stitches next to where the arm will join the body) (pics d, e, f).

With the needles parallel, knit through 2 stitches at once, creating 1 stitch (see *3-needle joining* pages 114–115). Once you have completed the 6 stitches on the front, wrap the arm around to the back and repeat the process for the back stitches.

Complete this process for the 2nd arm.

Stop when you have completed the 64th body rnd. Make sure you haven't stuffed right to the top as you will need room for sewing.

Sew on the eyes, nose and mouth using duplicate stitch for the eyes and nose, and a large, loose straight stitch with couching stitches for the smile (see *'embroidery stitches'* page 114), following the grid on page 77.

Continue with the decrease to shape and finish the head as per the Body with Legs instructions.

Ensure the body is stuffed to how firm or soft you want it before you close it up. See page 8 for tips on stuffing.

Make up

Hide any loose wool ends at the feet, head and arms (see *'hiding wool inside of body'* page 116).

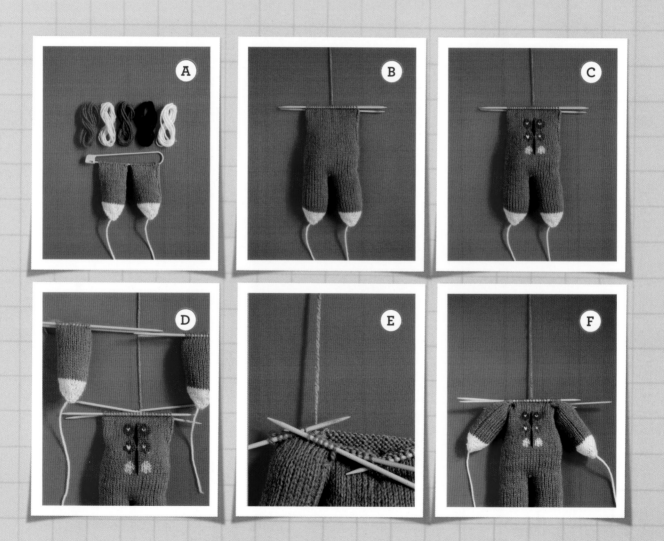

Gingerbread Man Buttons Grid

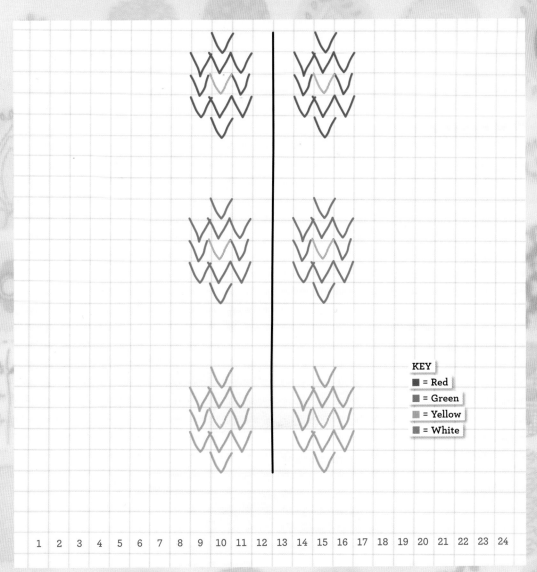

KEY
- ■ = Red
- ■ = Green
- ■ = Yellow
- ■ = White

| 1 | 2 | 3 | 4 | 5 | 6 | 7 | 8 | 9 | 10 | 11 | 12 | 13 | 14 | 15 | 16 | 17 | 18 | 19 | 20 | 21 | 22 | 23 | 24 |

Gingerbread Man Face Grid

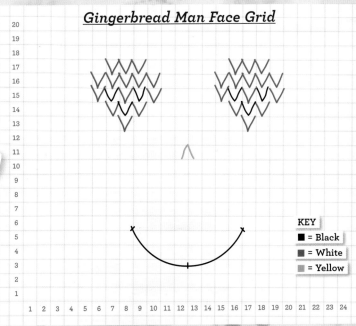

KEY
- ■ = Black
- ■ = White
- ■ = Yellow

SKIP THE ROBOT

"Beep boop boop beep my name is Skip
My brain is one big microchip! If you'd like to
watch a scene, I'll display it on my screen."

Personalise me!
*See page 68 for an alphabet grid to add initials
to the robot's screen.*

◇◇◇◇◇◇◇◇◇◇◇◇◇◇◇◇◇◇◇◇◇◇◇◇◇◇

Materials needed
4 x double-pointed 4mm needles
Wool (100g dark grey for body; 50g blue for legs
and screen; 50g yellow for legs, arms, eyes and
screen; 50g red for feet, mouth and antenna;
skein of black for screen and eye embroidery)
Scissors
Stitch holder
Wool needle
Pompom maker
Stuffing

◇◇◇◇◇◇◇◇◇◇◇◇◇◇◇◇◇◇◇◇◇◇◇◇◇◇

Skills needed
Casting on
Casting off
Knit stitch (K)
Purl stitch (P)
Knitting in the round
Increasing stitches (Inc 1)
Decreasing stitches (K2 tog, s1k1 psso)
Duplicate stitch embroidery
Changing colours
Transferring stitches to and from a stitch holder
Pompom making
Sewing

*If you are unfamiliar with any of these materials
or skills, turn to pages 6 and 112 for details.*

◇◇◇◇◇◇◇◇◇◇◇◇◇◇◇◇◇◇◇◇◇◇◇◇◇◇

Eyes
The eyes are knitted flat, using knit stitch for
each row to create a garter stitch. You only need
2 x 4mm needles.

Cast on 2 sts with the yellow wool. Make sure
you leave at least 12cm wool hanging so you
have enough to sew the eyes onto the face.

Knit 1 row.

Begin increase

2nd row: Inc 2, (4 sts).

Knit 1 row.

4th row: K1, inc 2, k1, (6 sts.)

Knit 4 rows.

Begin decrease

9th row: K1, s1k1 psso, k2 tog, k1, (4 sts).

Knit 1 row.

11th row: s1k1 psso, k2 tog (2 sts).

Knit 1 row.

Cast off.

Hide the loose wool end (see 'weaving method' page 116 for instructions).

Sew on the eyes using straight stitches (see 'embroidery stitches' page 114), following the grid on page 81.

Repeat for the 2nd eye.

Mouth

The mouth is also knitted flat, using knit stitch for each row to create a garter stitch. You only need 2 x 4mm needles.

Cast on 12 sts with the red wool, leaving at least 20cm wool hanging so you have enough to sew the mouth onto the face.

Knit 6 rows.

Cast off. Hide the wool end away (see 'weaving method' page 116 for instructions).

Arms

Using a pompom maker with a 60-70mm diameter (centre hole will be around 10mm) and the yellow wool, make 2 yellow pompoms. Refer to instructions 'making a pompom' on page 114.

Antenna

Using a pompom maker with a 40-50mm diameter (centre hole will be around 10mm) and the red wool, make 1 red pompom.

Screen

The screen is made of 2 rectangles, both knitted flat and sewn together for a 'frame' effect.

The larger blue rectangle, which creates the frame, is knitted in garter stitch (each row is knitted).

The smaller yellow rectangle, which creates the screen, is knitted in stocking stitch (alternating rows of knit and purl stitch).

You only need 2 x 4mm needles.

Leave at least 30cm wool hanging for each rectangle so you have enough to sew the yellow rectangle onto the blue rectangle, and then the blue rectangle onto the body.

Large rectangle

Cast on 20 sts with the blue wool.

Knit 28 rows.

Cast off. Hide the wool end away (see 'weaving method' page 116 for instructions).

Small rectangle

Cast on 15 sts with the yellow wool.

Beginning with a k row, work 12 rows stocking st (alternating rows of k and p), ending on a p row.

Cast off.

Using the black wool, sew on your chosen initials using duplicate stitch (see 'embroidery stitches' page 114), following the grid on page 68.

Body

Follow the instructions for the Body with Legs pattern on page 32, with the following modifications:

Feet

To make the feet, use a 3-needle joining and binding technique to create the edge (see page 115 for instructions).

The feet are knitted using more stitches than the Body with Legs pattern uses, but this is then reduced using the 3-needle joining and binding technique to create the leg. The knitting then continues with the standard number of stitches (24 sts).

Cast on 8 sts with the red wool.

Split the stitches over 3 needles (2-4-2).

Work 1 rnd.

2nd rnd: Inc 1 in every st, (4-8-4) 16 sts.

Work 1 rnd.

4th rnd: *K1, inc 1**, repeat *to** for the entire rnd, (6-12-6) 24 sts.

Work 1 rnd.

6th rnd: *K2, inc 1**, repeat *to** for the entire rnd, (8-16-8) 32 sts.

Work 1 rnd.

8th rnd: *K3, inc 1**, repeat *to** for the entire rnd, (10-20-10) 40 sts.

Work 1 rnd.

Lay the foot flat (see pic b). Place 12 sts from the front and 12 sts from the back needles (24 total) onto a stitch holder (pic b).

Reconfigure the remaining 16 stitches so they are split 8-8 across 2 parallel needles (pic c). This closes off these stitches to create the edge of the foot.

Holding these 2 needles parallel to one another, knit through 2 sts at once, creating 1 stitch on the opposite needle.

Once you have 2 sts on the needle, begin to cast off by pulling one st over the other.

Repeat this process until all 16 sts are joined and cast off.

Reconfigure the 24 sts on the stitch holder as per a leg from the Body with Legs pattern (page 32).

Work the leg as per the pattern, beginning by joining the blue wool (see '*joining new wool or changing colours*' page 116) and working for 8 rnds, then switching to yellow wool and working for 8 rnds. Finally, switch back to blue wool and work for another 8 rnds.

Once the legs are joined together, start the body using the dark grey wool.

Work 40 rnds dark grey.

Switch to light grey and work for the rest of the Body with Legs pattern in this colour.

Ensure the body is stuffed to how firm or soft you want it before you close it up. See page 8 for tips on stuffing.

Make up

Hide any loose wool ends at the feet and head (see '*hiding wool inside of body*' page 116).

Attach pompom arms on the sides of the body and antenna on top of the head (see '*sewing on pompoms and tassels*' page 117).

Sew on the eyes and mouth (see '*sewing onto your work*' page 116).

If not already done, sew the yellow screen onto the blue, ensuring it is centred. Sew the blue screen onto the body.

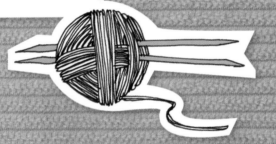

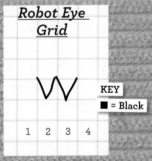

Robot Eye Grid

KEY
■ = Black

1 2 3 4

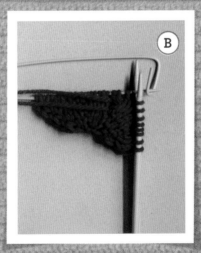

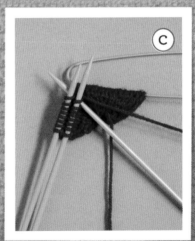

DIPLODOCUS DINO

Diplodocus is diplo-long, His tail and legs
are diplo-strong, You need not fear this dinosaur
'Cause he's a friendly herbivore.

Materials needed

4 x double-pointed 4mm needles
Wool (100g dark green for body and nose; 25g
light green for nostrils and foot; 25g yellow for
foot and eyes)
Scissors
Stitch holder
Wool needle
Stuffing

◇◇◇◇◇◇◇◇◇◇◇◇◇◇◇◇◇◇◇◇◇◇◇◇◇◇◇◇◇◇◇

Skills needed

Casting on
Casting off
Knit stitch (K)
Knitting in the round
Increasing stitches (Inc 1)
Decreasing stitches (K2 tog, s1k1 psso)
Changing colours
3-needle joining and binding
Sewing

*If you are unfamiliar with any of these materials
or skills, turn to pages 6 and 112 for details.*

◇◇◇◇◇◇◇◇◇◇◇◇◇◇◇◇◇◇◇◇◇◇◇◇◇◇◇◇◇◇◇

Nose

The nose is knitted flat, using knit stitch for
each row to create a garter stitch. You only
need 2 x 4mm needles.

Cast on 4 sts with the dark green wool. Make
sure you leave at least 12cm wool hanging so
you have enough to sew the nose onto the face.

Knit 1 row.

Begin increase

2nd row: K1, inc 1, inc 1, k1, (6 sts).

Knit 1 row.

4th row: K1, inc 1, k2, inc 1, k1, (8 sts).

Knit 3 rows.

Begin decrease

8th row: K1, s1k1 psso, k2, k2 tog, k1, (6 sts).

Knit 1 row.

10th row: K1, s1k1 psso, k2 tog, k1, (4 sts).

Cast off. Hide the wool end away as per the
'weaving method' instructions on page 116.

Sew on 2 nostrils using duplicate stitch (see
'embroidery stitches' page 114) following the
grid on page 87, using the light green wool.

Tail

Cast on 4 sts onto a 4mm double-pointed
needle using the dark green wool.

1st row: Inc 1 in every st, (8 sts).

Take these 8 sts and distribute them across
3 double-pointed needles (2-4-2).

Work 3 rnds

5th rnd: *K1, inc 1**, repeat *to** for the entire
rnd, (3-6-3) 12 sts.

Work 3 rnds.

9th rnd: *K2, inc 1**, repeat *to** for the entire rnd, (4-8-4) 16 sts.

Work 3 rnds.

13th rnd: *K3, inc 1**, repeat *to** for the entire rnd, (5-10-5) 20 sts.

Work 3 rnds.

17th rnd: *K4, inc 1**, repeat *to** for the entire rnd, (6-12-6) 24 sts.

Work these 24 stitches for 32 rnds.

Transfer onto a stitch holder.

Body

Follow the instructions for the Body with Legs pattern on page 32, with the following modifications:

One foot is done with a light green tip and the other foot is done with a yellow tip.

Stop after 8 body rnds to join the tail.

Attaching and shaping the tail

Remove the tail stitches from the stitch holder, redistributing them across the 3 needles with the existing stitches, (18-36-18) 72 sts (pic a).

9th rnd: K until you reach the point where the tail begins. (There should be 12 sts on the left needle, or right if you are left-handed). *K2 tog, k4**, repeat * to ** 3 more times, then k the rest of the rnd (16-34-18) 68 sts.

Work 1 rnd.

11th rnd: K until you reach the point where the tail begins. (There should be 10 sts on the left needle, or right if you are left-handed). *K2 tog, k3**, repeat * to ** 3 more times, then k the rest of the rnd, (14-32-18) 64 sts.

Work 1 rnd.

13th rnd: K until you reach the point where the tail begins. (There should be 8 sts on the left needle, or right if you are left-handed). *K2 tog, k2**, repeat * to ** 3 more times, then k the rest of the rnd, (12-30-18) 60 sts.

Work 1 rnd.

15th rnd K until you reach the point where the tail begins. (There should be 6 sts on the left needle, or right if you are left-handed). **K2 tog, k1**, repeat * to ** 3 more times, then k the rest of the rnd, (10-28-18) 56 sts.

Work 2 rnds.

18th rnd: K until you reach the point where the tail begins. (There should be 4 sts on the left needle, or right if you are left-handed). *K2 tog**, repeat * to ** 3 more times, then k the rest of the rnd, (8-26-18) 52 sts.

Work 2 rnds.

21st rnd: K until you reach the point where there is 2 sts before the tail begins. (There should be 4 sts on the left needle, or right if you are left-handed). *K2 tog**, repeat * to ** 3 more times, then k the rest of the rnd, (6-24-18) 48 sts.

Work 1 rnd.

Ensure the body is stuffed to how firm or soft you want it, leaving about 10mm loose at the top for closing off.

Shaping the back.

Lay the dinosaur flat so the front leg is on the right and the tail on the left.

Take 12 stitches from the front of each needle, above the front leg, and place these 24 stitches onto a stitch holder. Distribute the remaining 36 stitches evenly across 2 needles (18-18) (pic b).

Using the 3-needle joining and binding method (see page 115), take a 3rd needle and loosely knit into 2 sts at a time across the two needles (pic c).

Dinosaur Nose Grid

V   V

1 2 3 4 5 6 7 8

Each time there are 2 stitches on the right needle (left if you are left-handed) cast off 1 stitch. Repeat until all 36 stitches are cast off.

Transfer the remaining 24 stitches from the stitch holder onto 3 needles (6-12-6).

Work these 24 sts for 32 more rnds.

Before beginning to decrease, sew on the eyes, using duplicate stitch (see 'embroidery stitches' page 114), following the grid (right).

Ensure the neck is stuffed to how firm or soft you want it before you close it up.

Make up

Sew the nose on securely (see 'sewing onto your work' page 116).

Dinosaur Eye Grid

V   V

1 2 3 4 5 6 7 8 9 10 11 12

The tail is joined to the back of the body using decreasing stitches so it blends into the body, helping to create the back of the dinosaur (a). The tail half of the body shape is knitted closed, creating the back (b, c), and the remaining body half is worked into a long neck shape for the dinosaur.

A

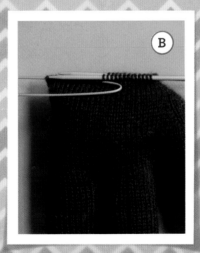

B

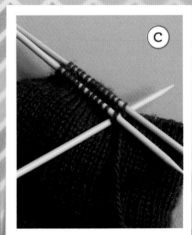

C

BABY GIRAFFE

Baby giraffe's entrance is grand, Within an hour
she can stand, Within twelve her strides are deep,
Within a day she's fast asleep.

Materials needed

4 x double-pointed 4mm needles
Wool (100g yellow for body, tail and ears;
50g medium brown for mane, horn tips, tail,
feet and pattern detail; small skeins of black
and green for eyes)
Scissors
Stitch holder
Wool needle
Pompom maker
Stuffing
French knitting tool
Crochet hook (optional but recommended)

Skills needed

Casting on
Casting off
Knit stitch (K)
Knitting in the round
Increasing stitches (Inc 1)
Decreasing stitches (K2 tog, s1k1 psso)
Changing colours
Strand knitting
Pompom making
3-needle joining and binding
Sewing

*If you are unfamiliar with any of these materials
or skills, turn to pages 6 and 112 for details.*

Nose

The nose is knitted flat, using knit stitch for
each row to create a garter stitch. You only
need 2 x 4mm needles.

Cast on 4 sts with the medium brown wool,
leaving at least 12cm wool hanging so you
have enough to sew the nose onto the face.

Knit 1 row.

Begin increase

2nd row: K1, inc 1, inc 1, k1. (6 sts).

Knit 1 row.

4th row: K1, inc 1, k2, inc 1, k1. (8 sts).

Knit 3 rows.

Begin decrease

8th row: K1, s1k1 psso, k2, k2 tog, k1. (6 sts).

Knit 1 row.

10th row: K1, s1k1 psso, k2 tog, k1. (4 sts).

Cast off. Hide wool end away (see *'weaving
method'* page 116 for instructions).

Sew on 2 nostrils using duplicate stitch (see
'embroidery stitches' page 114), following the
grid on page 92 and using the yellow wool.

Ears

The ears are also knitted flat, using knit stitch for each row to create a garter stitch. You only need 2 x 4mm needles.

Cast on 8 sts with the yellow wool, leaving 12cm wool hanging after casting on as you will use this to finish the ears and sew them to the giraffe's head.

*Knit 1 row.

2nd row: S1k1 psso, k to last 2 sts, k2 tog**, (6 sts).

Repeat * to ** until 2 stitches remain.

Knit 1 row.

8th row: Pass 1 st over the other (1 st).

Cut the wool, leaving at least 10cm hanging. Thread a wool needle and pull the loose end through the remaining stitch, then hide the end away (see '*weaving method*' instructions on page 116.

Pinch the ear together to create a more pointed and angled effect. Refer to *Wobbly Wombat* 'Ears' page 16, and pics b, c page 17, on how to sew up the ear. Repeat this process to make the 2nd ear.

Mane

Using a pompom maker with a 40-50mm diameter (centre hole will be around 10mm) and the medium brown wool, make 5 pompoms. Refer to instructions '*making a pompom*' on page 114.

Horn tips

Using a pompom maker with a 25mm diameter (centre hole will be around 10mm) and the medium brown wool, make 2 pompoms.

Tail

Using the yellow wool and the French knitting technique (see page 115 for instructions), create a cord that is 60mm in length. Place the 4 stitches on a stitch holder.

Using a pompom maker with a 25mm diameter (centre hole will be around 10mm) and the brown wool, make 1 medium brown pompom.

Sew the pompom onto one end of the tail (see '*sewing on pompoms and tassels*' page 117).

Body

Follow the instructions for the Body with Legs pattern on page 32, with the following modifications:

Spots

To mimic the giraffe's spots, introduce medium brown wool stitches following the pattern on the grid on page 91 (pics b, c). This technique is known as Strand or Fair Isle knitting (see page 115).

Switch to the main (M) colour wool (yellow) on the legs, work 4 rnds.

5th rnd: Introduce brown wool as per grid.

Work 4 rnds yellow.

10th rnd: Introduce brown wool as per grid.

Work this pattern for 24 leg rnds.

Once the legs are joined to the body, continue with this pattern.

Joining the tail

Stop after 22 body rnds to join the tail.

Remove tail from the stitch holder and add to the end of 2 needles (12-26-14) 52 sts (pic d, page 92).

Work 1 rnd.

24th rnd: K until you reach the point where the tail begins. K2 tog, k2 tog, k to the end of the round (50 sts).

Work 1 rnd.

26th rnd: K until you reach the point where the tail begins (see photo). K2 tog, k2 tog, k to the end of the round (48 sts).

Ensure the body is stuffed to how firm or soft you want it, leaving about 10mm loose at the top for closing off.

Shaping the back

Lay the giraffe flat so the front leg is on the right and the tail on the left.

Take 12 stitches from the front of each needle, above the front leg; place these 24 stitches onto a stitch holder. Distribute the remaining 36 stitches evenly across 2 needles (18-18) (pic e).

Using the 3-needle joining and binding method (see page 112), take a 3rd needle and very loosely knit into 2 stitches at a time across the two needles (pic f) to make 1 stitch.

Every time there are 2 stitches on the right needle (left if you are left-handed) cast off 1 stitch. Repeat until all 36 sts are cast off.

Transfer the remaining 24 stitches from the stitch holder onto 3 needles (6-12-6).

Work these 24 sts for 36 rnds following grid below.

Before beginning the decrease, sew on the eyes, using duplicate stitch (see '*embroidery stitches*' page 114), following the grid on page 92.

Shaping the horns

Take 12 sts (6 from the left front and 6 from the left back) and place them on a stitch holder. Reconfigure the three needles (3-6-3) with the 6-stitch needle across the front.

37th rnd: *K1, k2 tog**, repeat *to** for the entire rnd, (2-4-2) 8 sts.

Work 1 rnd.

39th: *K2 tog**, repeat *to** for the entire rnd, (1-2-1) 4 sts.

Cut the wool leaving around 10cm. Thread a wool needle and pass it through these 4 sts as you pull them off the needle.

Transfer stitches from stitch holder and place them across 3 needles (3-6-3) as per the first horn. Repeat these steps for the 2nd horn.

Ensure the horns are stuffed to how firm or soft you want them before finishing the second horn.

Make up

Sew the nose on securely (see '*sewing onto your work*' page 116). Sew ears onto either side of the head. Sew up the small gap between the horns.

Sew a small pompom on the top of each horn (see '*sewing on pompoms and tassels*' page 117). Sew on 5 brown pompoms for the mane, beginning at the top of the head and spacing them about 10mm-15mm apart.

Giraffe spots

KEY
■ = Brown

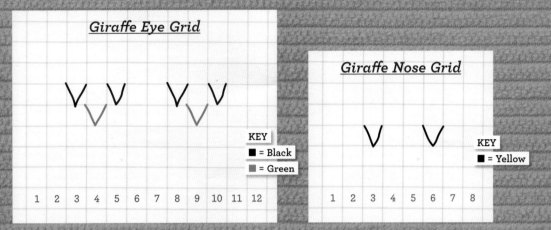

Giraffe Eye Grid

KEY
■ = Black
■ = Green

1 2 3 4 5 6 7 8 9 10 11 12

Giraffe Nose Grid

KEY
■ = Yellow

1 2 3 4 5 6 7 8

When making the giraffe's 'spots', carry the brown wool with the yellow wool as you knit. This causes a lot of loose strands and, while it may look messy, it is normal for this type of knitting (b, c). If you find the strands too challenging, make the giraffe without the 'spots'. Or, have a look at the robot eye pattern (page 78) or the gorilla chest pattern (page 94) – you could knit some of these to sew onto the giraffe.

SILVERBACK GORILLA

In the mountains of the Congo, Beats his chest
loud like a bongo, And his friends all dance and sing
With their silver hairy king.

Materials needed

6 x double-pointed 4mm needles
Wool (100g black; 50g light grey; 50g dark grey)
Scissors
Stitch holder
Wool needle
Stuffing
Lightly dampened towel or cloth
Iron

◇◇◇◇◇◇◇◇◇◇◇◇◇◇◇◇◇◇◇◇◇◇◇◇◇

Skills needed

Casting on
Casting off
Knit stitch (K)
Purl stitch (P)
Knitting in the round
Increasing stitches (Inc 1)
Decreasing stitches (K2 tog, s1k1 psso)
Changing colours
Duplicate stitch embroidery
Transferring stitches to and from a stitch holder
3-needle joining
Sewing

*If you are unfamiliar with any of these materials
or skills, turn to pages 6 and 112 for details.*

Arms

The arms are made exactly as per a leg (see
page 32), except work for 48 rnds instead of 24.

We used light grey as our contrast colour for the tip
of one arm and dark grey for the tip of the other.

Ensure the arm is stuffed, leaving around 10mm
unstuffed at the top where the needles are.

Close off the arms so there is one row of stitches.
This allows the arms to be knitted directly onto
the body.

To do this, use the 3-needle joining method (see
page 114 for instructions).

Face

The face is knitted flat, using knit and purl stitches
on alternating rows to create stocking stitch. You
only need 2 x 4mm needles.

Cast on 8 sts with the dark grey wool, leaving at
least 20cm wool hanging so you have enough to
sew the face onto the body.

1st row: P

Begin decrease

2nd row: K1, inc 1, k2, inc 1, k1, (10 sts).

3rd row: P

4th row: K1, inc 1, k4, inc 1, k1, (12 sts).

Work 7 rows stocking st, finishing after a p row.

Begin decrease

12th row: K1, s1k1 psso, k10, k2 tog, k1, (10 sts).

17th row: P

18th row: K

19th row: P

Cast off.

Sew on the eyes and nostrils using duplicate stitch and the mouth and brow using straight stitch (see '*embroidery stitches*' page 114), following the grid on page 97 (pic b).

Stomach

The stomach is knitted flat, using knit and purl stitches on alternating rows to create stocking stitch. You only need 2 x 4mm needles.

Cast on 14 sts with the dark grey wool, leaving at least 20cm wool hanging so you have enough to sew the face onto the body.

1st row: *P

2nd row: K1, inc 1, knit to last 2 sts, inc 1, k1**, (16 sts).

Repeat *to**, (18 sts).

Work stocking stitch for 15 rows, finishing after a purl row.

Begin decrease

20th row: *K1, s1k1 psso, k to last 3 sts, k2 tog, k1 (16 sts).

Purl 1 row**

Repeat *to** once, (14 sts).

Cast off.

Sew on the belly button using duplicate stitches (see '*embroidery stitches*' page 114) following the grid on page 99.

Chest

The chest muscles are knitted flat, using knit and purl stitches on alternating rows to create stocking stitch. You only need 2 x 4mm needles.

Cast on 6 sts with the dark grey wool, leaving at least 12cm wool hanging so you have enough to sew the face onto the body.

1st row: P

Begin increase

2nd row: K1, inc 1, k to last 2 sts, inc 1, k1, (8 sts).

Work stocking stitch for 3 rows, finishing after a purl row.

Begin decrease

6th row: K1, s1k1 psso, k to last 3 sts, k2 tog, k1, (6 sts).

7th row: P

Cast off.

Repeat for 2nd chest muscle (pic c).

Sew nipples into the chest using duplicate stitches (see '*embroidery stitches*' page 114) following the grid on page 99.

Legs

Make 2 legs as per the instructions for Body with Legs pattern on page 32, using dark grey for the contrast (C) colour and black for the (M) main colour. Place 24 stitches onto a stitch holder. Place remaining 24 stitches onto one needle (these stitches will become the gorilla's back).

Body

Note: Don't stuff the gorilla as you go, as recommended for other animals. He will be stuffed when making up.

Making the silver back

Join the light grey wool, and work the 24 stitches (for the gorilla's back) in stocking stitch. Ensure the right (knit) side is aligned with the legs (pics d, e).

Work 39 rows.

Transfer these 24 stitches onto a stitch holder.

Take the 24 black stitches from the stitch holder and transfer them onto a needle (pic f).

Work in stocking stitch with black wool, with the right side facing the opposite to the light grey.

Work 39 rows.

Remove the light grey stitches from the stitch holder; reconfigure all the stitches across the 3 needles (12-24-12) so you are knitting in the round.

Work 1 rnd with the black wool.

Joining the arms

Join the arms using the 3-needle joining method (see pages 114-115).

The arms should be centred either side of the body, so align the arm stitches with 6 stitches from the front and 6 stitches from the back needles.

40th rnd: Work 40th rnd, but stop 6 sts from the end of the front needle; take the needle with the first arm and lie this parallel to the working needle (aligning the 12 arm stitches with the 6 front stitches next to where the arm will join the body (pic g).

With the needles parallel, knit through 2 stitches at once, creating 1 stitch (see *3-needle joining* pages 114-115). Once you have completed the 6 stitches on the front, wrap the arm around to the back and repeat the process for the back stitches (pics h, i, j).

Complete this process for the 2nd arm.

Work 23 rnds with the black wool.

Begin decrease to form head

64th rnd: *K4, k2 tog**, repeat *to** for the entire rnd, (10-20-10) 40 sts.

Work 1 rnd.

66th rnd: *K3, k2 tog**, repeat *to** for the entire rnd, (8-16-8) 32 sts.

Work 1 rnd.

68th rnd: *K2, k2 tog**, repeat *to** for the entire rnd, (6-12-6) 24 sts.

Work 1 rnd.

70th rnd: *K1, k2 tog**, repeat *to** for the entire rnd, (4-8-4) 16 sts.

Work 1 rnd.

72nd rnd: K2 tog for the entire rnd, (2-4-2) 8 sts.

Cut the wool leaving around 16cm. Thread a wool needle and pass it through these 8 sts as you pull them off the needle. Pull the loose end tightly to close the stitches.

Make up

Hide any loose wool ends at the feet, arms and head (see *'hiding wool inside of body'* page 116 for instructions).

Lay the face, chest and stomach flat under a lightly dampened clean tea towel; press with an iron set to the wool setting, or to three-quarters of maximum.

Sew one side of the body together using mattress stitch (see page 114) (pic k). With the other side still open, stuff the body to the desired firmness (pic l). Sew the sides together.

Sew the face, chest and stomach to the body (see *'sewing onto your work'* page 116).

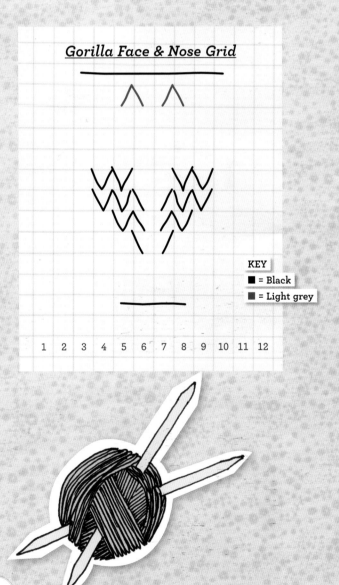

Gorilla Face & Nose Grid

KEY
■ = Black
■ = Light grey

1 2 3 4 5 6 7 8 9 10 11 12

Gorilla Chest Grid

| 1 | 2 | 3 | 4 | 5 | 6 |

KEY
■ = Black

| 1 | 2 | 3 | 4 | 5 | 6 |

Gorilla Belly Button Grid

KEY
■ = Black

| 1 | 2 | 3 | 4 | 5 | 6 | 7 | 8 | 9 | 10 | 11 | 12 | 13 | 14 | 15 | 16 |

NAPOLEON PENGUIN

Penguin's look is very fine

It's a dapper natural design, A formal he need

not forego, He's always in a tuxedo!

Materials needed

6 x double-pointed 4mm needles
Wool (100g black for body and flippers;
50g white for tummy and flippers; 25g orange
for feet; skeins of blue and heather grey for the
eyes and beak)
Scissors
Stitch holder
Wool needle
Stuffing
Lightly dampened towel or cloth
Iron

Skills needed

Casting on
Casting off
Knit stitch (K)
Purl stitch (P)
Knitting in the round
Increasing stitches (Inc 1)
Decreasing stitches (K2 tog, s1k1 psso)
Knitting with two colours
Transferring stitches to and from a stitch holder
3-needle joining and binding
Mattress stitch
Sewing

If you are unfamiliar with any of these materials
or skills, turn to pages 6 and 112 for details.

Flippers

The flippers are knitted flat, using knit and purl
stitches on alternating rows to create stocking
stitch. You only need 2 x 4mm needles.

You will knit using 2 different colours on one
needle to create the black front and the white
inside of the flipper. This means that you won't
have to sew the flippers together later and
ensures both sides are identical, which makes
it much easier to finish up.

Cast on 8 sts with the main (M) wool, then cast
on 8 sts with the contrast (C) wool, wrapping the
contrast strand around the main strand before
you begin to join the 2 wools (see *knitting with*
2 colours side-by-side page 114). The technique is
similar to knitting the bunny's ears on page 38 as
this is the exact same pattern (pics b, c, page 39).

1st row: *P to end, switching from C to M where
the divide occurs. Continue to do this for the rest
of the flipper.

2nd row: K to end.

3rd row: P to end**.

Repeat * to ** until you have 7 rows.

Begin decrease

***8th row:** With the right side facing, s1k1 psso,
k to last 2 sts, k2 tog (14 sts – 7 M, 7 C).

Work 7 more rows stocking st**.

Repeat * to ** until 6 sts (3 M, 3 C) remain.

Cast off.

Cut the (M) wool leaving at least 30cm hanging to sew the edge together.

Cut the (C) wool leaving around 50mm hanging, which will be hid inside the folded flipper.

Repeat this process for the 2nd flipper. Put aside to attach to the body when complete.

Beak

The beak is also knitted flat, using knit stitch for each row to create a garter stitch. You only need 2 x 4mm needles.

Cast on 8 sts with the heather grey wool, leaving at least 14cm wool hanging so you have enough to sew the beak onto the face.

Knit 2 rows.

Begin decrease

3rd row: S1k1 psso, k4, k2 tog, (6 sts).

Knit 2 rows.

6th row: S1k1 psso, k2, k2 tog, (4 sts).

Knit 2 rows.

9th row: S1k1 psso, k2, k2 tog, (2 sts).

Knit 2 rows.

Cast off.

Hide the wool end away as per the '*weaving method*' instructions on page 116.

Feet

To make the feet, use the 3-needle joining and binding technique to create the edge (see page 115 for instructions). (See also pics b, c for creating the robot's feet on page 81 as this is the same pattern.)

Cast on 8 sts using the orange wool.

Split stitches over 3 needles (2-4-2).

Work 1 rnd.

2nd rnd: Inc 1 in every st, (16 sts).

Work 1 rnd.

4th rnd: *K1, inc 1**, repeat *to** for the entire rnd, (6-12-6) 24 sts.

Work 1 rnd.

6th rnd: *K2, inc 1**, repeat *to** for the entire rnd, (8-16-8) 32 sts.

Work 1 rnd.

8th rnd: *K3, inc 1**, repeat *to** for the entire rnd, (10-20-10) 40 sts.

Work 1 rnd.

Lay the foot flat. Transfer 12 stitches from the front and 12 stitches from the back needles (24 sts) onto a stitch holder.

Reconfigure the remaining 16 stitches so they are split 8-8 across 2 parallel needles (see pics b, c page 81). You will be closing off these stitches to create the edge of the foot.

With the needles parallel, knit through 2 stitches at once, creating 1 stitch (see *3-needle joining* pages 114-115). Once you have 2 stitches on the needle, begin to cast off by pulling 1 st over the other.

Repeat this process until all 16 sts are joined and cast off.

Repeat this process for the 2nd foot.

Body

Note: Don't stuff the penguin as you go, as recommended for the other animals; it will be stuffed during the making up stage.

Remove the feet from the stitch holders and place across 3 needles (12-24-12) (pic b).

Attach black wool (see *'joining new wool or changing colours'* page 116) (pic c).

Work 2 rnds.

Transfer 24 stitches from the two 12-st needles plus one stitch from each end of the 24-st needle onto a stitch holder, leaving 22 sts on 1 needle. (This is similar to pic d, on page 98, except using 22 sts instead of 24).

With the white wool, knit these 22 sts in stocking stitch. Ensure that the right (knit) side is facing out.

Work 56 rows.

Transfer these 22 sts onto a stitch holder (pic d).

Transfer the remaining 26 black stitches from the stitch holder onto a needle.

Work in stocking stitch with the black wool, with the right (knit) side facing opposite the white wool.

Work for 56 rows.

Transfer the white stitches from the stitch holder and reconfigure all the stitches across 3 needles (12-24-12) so you are knitting in the round (pic e).

Work 24 rnds with black wool.

Sew on the eyes using duplicate stitch (see *'embroidery stitches'* page 114) following the grid on page 104.

Begin decrease to form head

81st rnd: *K4, k2 tog**, repeat *to** for the entire rnd, (10-20-10) 40 sts.

Work 1 rnd.

83rd: *K3, k2 tog**, repeat *to** for the entire rnd, (8-16-8) 32 sts.

Work 1 rnd.

85th rnd: *K2, k2 tog**, repeat *to** for the entire rnd, (6-12-6) 24 sts.

Work 1 rnd.

87th rnd: *K1, k2 tog**, repeat *to** for the entire rnd, (4-8-4) 16 sts.

Work 1 rnd.

89th rnd: K2 tog for the entire rnd, (2-4-2) 8 sts.

You have finished the body.

Cut the wool leaving around 16cm. Thread a wool needle and pass it through these 8 sts as you pull them off the needle.

Pull the loose end tightly to close the stitches.

Make up

Hide any loose wool ends at the feet and head (see *'hiding wool inside of body'* page 116 for instructions).

Sew one side of the body together using mattress stitch (see page 114). With the other side still open, stuff the body to your desired firmness. Sew the other side together (pic f).

Lay the flippers flat under a lightly dampened clean tea towel; press with an iron set to wool setting. If the iron doesn't have a wool setting, set the heat dial to three-quarters of maximum.

Using mattress stitch, sew up the side and top with the M wool. Ensure the contrast wool is hidden inside the flipper.

Sew on the beak (see *'sewing onto your work'* page 116).

Sew both flippers evenly onto the sides of the body at the same level where the white tummy ends.

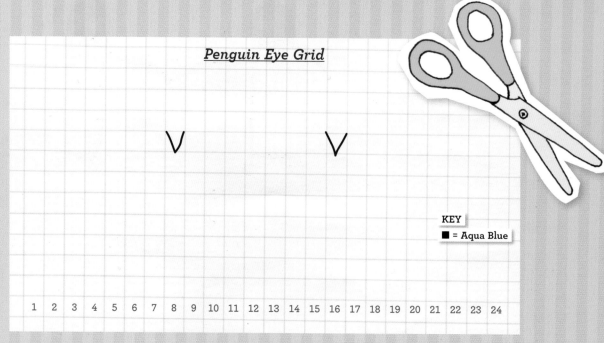

Penguin Eye Grid

KEY
■ = Aqua Blue

| 1 | 2 | 3 | 4 | 5 | 6 | 7 | 8 | 9 | 10 | 11 | 12 | 13 | 14 | 15 | 16 | 17 | 18 | 19 | 20 | 21 | 22 | 23 | 24 |

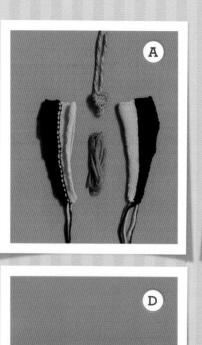

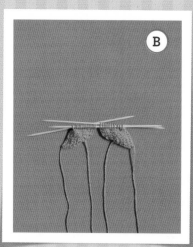

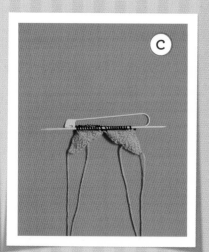

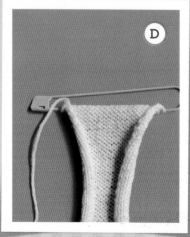

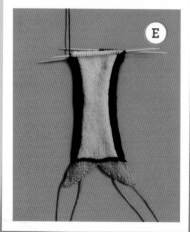

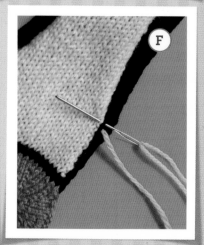

SLEEPY SHARK

He swims around the ocean deep, His presence makes the
others weep, And wail and shout and splash about
When all he wants to do is sleep!

Materials needed

6 x 4mm double-pointed needles
2 x 3.25mm double-pointed needles
Wool needle
Stitch holder
Scissors
Wool (100g dark grey main; 50g light grey
for stomach and fins; 50g black for mouth and
eyes; 25g white for teeth;
skein red for gums)
Stuffing
Lightly dampened towel or cloth
Iron

Skills needed

Casting on
Casting off
Knit stitch (K)
Purl stitch (P)
Knitting in the round
Increasing stitches (Inc 1)
Decreasing stitches (K2 tog, s1k1 psso)
Knitting with two colours
3-needle joining and binding
Changing colours
Transferring stitches to and from a stitch holder
Mattress stitch
Sewing

*If you are unfamiliar with any of these materials
or skills, turn to pages 6 and 112 for details.*

Note: Don't stuff the shark as you go, as
recommended for the other animals. He
will be stuffed during the making up stage.

Side fins

The side fins are knitted flat, using knit and purl
stitches on alternating rows to create stocking
stitch. You only need 2 x 4mm needles.

The fins are knitted using 2 different colours on
one needle to create the grey-coloured outer fin
and the light grey-coloured inner fin.

Cast on 12 sts with the main (M) wool, then cast
on 12 sts with the contrast (C) wool, wrapping
the contrast strand around the main strand
before you begin to join the 2 wools (see *knitting
with 2 colours side-by-side* page 114) (pic b).

1st row: *P to end, switching from C to M where
the divide occurs. Continue to do this for the rest
of the fin.

2nd row: S1k1 psso, k to last 2 sts, k2 tog (22 sts).

Next row: P**

Repeat * to ** until 2 stitches remain.

Cast off.

Repeat this process for the 2nd fin, but reverse
the order of the greys so that the fins are mirror
images of each other.

Dorsal fin

Use the same steps for the side fins to make the
dorsal fin; however, make only one dorsal fin.

Mouth interior

The mouth interior is knitted flat, using knit and purl stitches on alternating rows to create stocking stitch. You only need 2 x 4mm needles.

Cast on 2 sts using black wool.

1st row: P

2nd row: Inc 1 both sts (4 sts)

3rd row: *P

4th row, Inc 1, knit to the last st, inc 1** (6 sts).

Repeat from * to ** until there are 22 sts.

21st row: Beginning with a p row, work 5 rows stocking sts.

Begin decrease

26th row: *S1k1 psso, k until last 2 sts, k2 tog, (20 sts).

Next row: P **

Repeat from * to ** until 2 stitches remain.

Cast off.

Teeth

The teeth are knitted flat, using knit stitch every row to create garter stitch. To create the individual points for the teeth you need to leave the work on one long needle while you work each individual tooth, 4 sts at a time, casting off 2 sts in-between each tooth.

Cast on 96 sts onto the 3.25mm double-pointed needles using dark red wool.

1st row: Switch to white wool (see '*joining new wool or changing colours*' page 116) and k1 row.

*With the 3rd 3.25mm needle, k4 sts. Turn the main needle and knit only these 4 sts for 2 more rows (pic c).

Next row: S1k1 psso, k2 tog, (2 sts).

Knit 1 row.

7th row: K2 tog. Cut the wool. Thread a wool needle with the loose end and pull through the other loop. You have completed one tooth. Re-attach the white wool and cast off the next 2 sts**.

Repeat * to ** 15 times (pic d) to make 16 teeth in total. Weave loose ends into the teeth to hide them (see the '*weaving method*' instructions on page 116).

Tail fins

To make the fins, use the 3-needle joining and binding technique to create the edge (see page 115 for instructions). (See also pics b, c for creating the robot's feet on page 81 as this is the same pattern.)

Cast on 8 sts using the dark grey wool.

Split stitches over 3 needles (2-4-2).

Work 1 rnd.

2nd rnd: Inc 1 in every st, (16 sts).

Work 1 rnd.

4th rnd: *K1, inc 1**, repeat *to** for the entire rnd, (6-12-6) 24 sts.

Work 1 rnd.

6th rnd: *K2, inc 1**, repeat *to** for the entire rnd, (8-16-8) 32 sts.

Work 1 rnd.

8th rnd: *K3, inc 1**, repeat *to** for the entire rnd, (10-20-10) 40 sts.

Work 1 rnd.

Lay the fin flat. Transfer 12 stitches from the front and 12 stitches from the back (24 sts) onto a stitch holder.

Reconfigure the remaining 16 stitches so they are split 8-8 across 2 parallel needles You will close off these stitches to create the edge of the fin (see pics b, c page 81).

With the needles parallel, knit through 2 stitches at once, creating 1 stitch (see *3-needle joining* pages 114-115). Once you have 2 stitches on the needle, begin to cast off by pulling 1 st over the other.

Repeat this process until all 16 sts are joined and cast off.

Repeat this process for the 2nd fin.

Body

Remove the tail fins from the stitch holders and place across 3 needles (12-24-12) (pic e). Attach the dark grey wool (see '*joining new wool or changing colours*' page 116).

Work 2 rnds.

Transfer the stitches from both the 12-stitch needles plus 1 stitch from each end of the 24-stitch needle onto a stitch holder, leaving 22 stitches on the larger needle.

Join the lighter grey wool, and work these 22 sts in stocking stitch. Ensure the right (knit) side is aligned with the tail fins (pic e).

Work 48 rows.

Begin shaping the mouth

*With the right side facing, s1k1 psso, k until 2 sts remain, k2 tog, (20 sts).

Next row: P **

Repeat * to ** until 2 stitches remain.

Cast off.

Transfer the remaining 26 stitches from the stitch holder onto a needle. Rejoin the wool and work in stocking stitch with the right (knit) side facing the opposite to the light grey for 48 rows (pic f).

With the right side facing, k1 row and then cast on 22 stitches onto the end of this row (pic g).

To cast on, use a 2nd ball of wool of the same colour to create the stitches and then use the existing wool to knit through them. Take these 48 sts and split them across 3 needles (12-24-12) (pic h).

Work 18 rnds.

Begin shaping the head

19th rnd: *K4, k2 tog**, repeat * to ** for 1 rnd, (10-20-10) 40 sts.

Work 3 rnds.

23rd rnd: *K3, k2 tog**, repeat * to ** for 1 rnd, (8-16-8) 32 sts.

Work 3 rnds

27th rnd: *K2, k2 tog**, repeat * to ** for 1 rnd, (6-12-6) 24 sts.

Work 3 rnds.

Sew on the eyes using duplicate stitch (see '*embroidery stitches*' page 114), following the grid on page 110.

31st rnd: *K1, k2 tog**, repeat * to ** for 1 rnd, (4-8-4) 16 sts.

Work 2 rnds.

34th rnd: *K2 tog**, repeat * to ** for 1 rnd, (2-4-2) 8 sts.

Cut the wool leaving around 16cm. Thread a wool needle and pass it through these 8 sts as you pull them off the needle. Pull the loose end tightly to close the stitches.

Make up

Hide any loose wool ends (see '*hiding wool inside of body*' page 116 for instructions.

Fins

Lay the side fins and dorsal fins flat under a lightly dampened clean tea towel; press with an iron set to wool setting. If the iron doesn't have a wool setting, set the heat dial to three-quarters of maximum.

Using mattress stitch (see page 114), use the main colour to sew up the side and top (ensure the contrast wool is hidden inside once the fins are made up).

Mouth

Take the string of teeth and line up with the red gum line around the edge of the mouth interior. Sew the gum line to the outside edge of the mouth with red wool and your wool needle. See '*sewing onto your work*' page 116.

Body

Sew on the eyes using duplicate stitch (see '*embroidery stitches*' page 114) following the grid page 110.

Sew both sides together using mattress stitch (see pic f, page 104).

Stuff the body to the desired firmness through the hole in the mouth.

Fold light grey triangular mouth flap down (pic i). Lay the mouth interior on top of the flap, lining up the corner and sides precisely so that the red gum line is visible on the outer edge of the mouth flap. Sew the mouth onto the body in this position.

Sew both side fins evenly onto the sides of the body around two-thirds from the top.

Sew the dorsal fin onto the centre of his back.

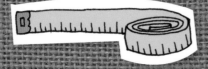

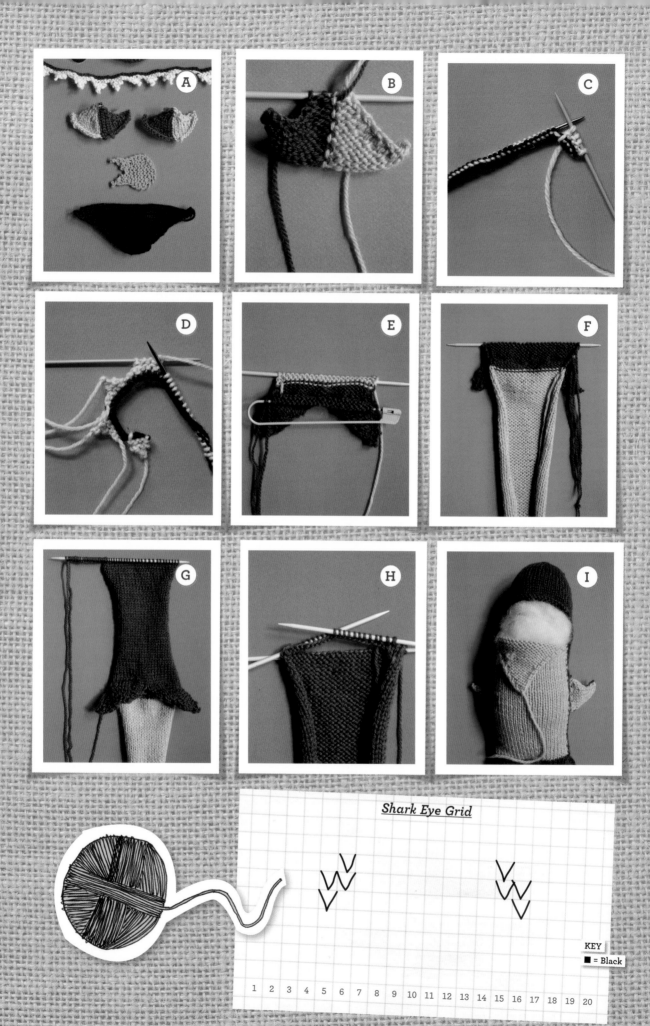

A

B

C

D

E

F

G

H

I

Shark Eye Grid

KEY
■ = Black

1 2 3 4 5 6 7 8 9 10 11 12 13 14 15 16 17 18 19 20

1. Casting on
Make a slipknot for the first stitch

a. Make a circle with the wool. There will be two ends – the wool attached to the ball (working wool) and the loose end (wool length). Ensure the wool length has 18cm for every 10 stitches you will cast on to the 4mm needles.
b. Take the working end and loop it behind the circle so it looks like a little pretzel.
c. Put the needle end through the bottom half of the circle, behind the working wool.
d. Gently pull both ends below the needle – a loop will form on the needle. This is the first stitch.

<u>c.</u>

<u>d.</u>

Casting on the remaining stitches

e. Hold the needle with the slip knot in the right hand (left hand if you are left-handed), take the wool length and wrap it around the back of the thumb on the opposite hand.
f. Take the needle up through the centre of the loop around the thumb.
g. Wrap the working wool around the needle and draw through the loop on the thumb.

h. Pull both wool ends firmly to create a new loop on the needle. Repeat until the required amount of stitches are on the needle.

f.

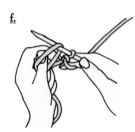

g.

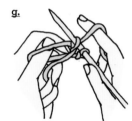

h.

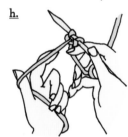

2. Casting off
a. Knit two stitches.
b (1). Using the left needle (or right if you are left-handed) pull the first stitch over the second stitch.

b (1).

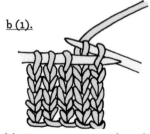

b (2). Knit one more stitch so that there are two stitches again on the opposite needle.
c. Once again pull the first stitch over the second stitch.

b (2).

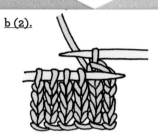

d. Repeat this process until there is only one stitch left.
e. To finish, cut the wool, leaving a generous end (most patterns in this book recommend a certain length). Thread this end with a wool needle, pull the end through the final stitch and pull tightly.

3. Knit stitch
a. Hold the needle with the cast on stitches in your hand (or right if you are left-handed).
b. Push the right (left) hand needle through the first stitch, from front to back, ensuring the working wool is behind the needle going through. Wind the working wool under the opposite needle then over the top and backwards to form a loop.
c. Pull this loop through the first stitch.
d. Slip the first stitch off the left (right) needle and onto the opposite needle.
e. Repeat steps for each stitch.

<u>b.</u>

<u>c.</u>

<u>d.</u>

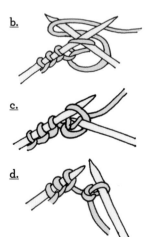

4. Purl stitch

a. Hold the needle with the cast on stitches in your left hand (or right if you are left-handed).
b. Push the right (left) hand needle through the first stitch, from back to front, ensuring the working wool is in front of the needle going through. Wind the working wool over the opposite needle then underneath to form a loop.
c. Pull this loop through the first stitch.
d. Slip the first stitch off the left (right) needle and onto the opposite needle.
e. Repeat steps for each stitch.

b.

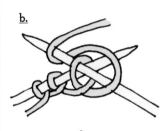

c.

d.

5. Knitting in the round

All of the patterns in this book require you to knit in the round – which means you have the stitches spit across three needles to form a triangle – you work all the stitches around the triangle so that you are creating a tube.

Knitting in the round allows you to create a stocking stitch by knitting every round, and requires much less making up as there are no sides to sew together.

While this may seem intimidating, once you get started it is no different to regular knitting – you just need to get comfortable with the configuration of the needles.

a. Cast all of the stitches onto one needle.
b. Slip the stitches onto two other needles as the pattern dictates. For example, many of our patterns will start out with 8 stitches and have you split these across three needles, 2-4-2.
c. Take these three needles and form a triangle.
d. Take a fourth needle and knit across the stitches on the first needle in the triangle. After you have finished knitting these stitches you will have a new empty needle.
e. With the new empty needle, knit across the stitches on the next needle in the triangle.
f. Repeat this pattern.

b.

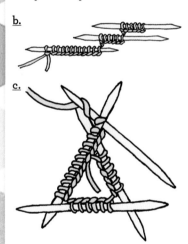

c.

Tip: *Knit the first couple of stitches on each new needle very tightly to prevent gaps – these are called ladders and are common when knitting in the round.*

6. Increasing stitches (Inc 1)

This method of increasing is called the Bar Increase:

a. Knit the stitch but leave it on the needle.
b. Knit once more into the back of this same stitch then slip it onto the opposite needle.

a.

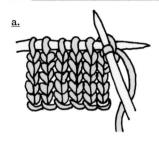

b.

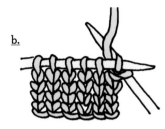

7. Decreasing stitches – Knit two together (K2 tog)

a. Slip the needle through two stitches instead of one, exactly as you would do if you were knitting into one stitch.
b. Knit both of these stitches together at the same time to create just one stitch.

a.

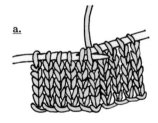

8. Decreasing stitches – Slip one knit one pass slipped stitch over (S1k1 psso)

a. Slip one stitch onto the opposite needle as if to knit but without actually knitting it.
b. Knit the following stitch.
c. Pull the slipped stitch back over the stitch you have just knit (it's the same process as when you are casting off).

c.

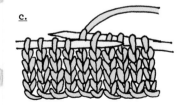

9. Embroidery stitches

To add details to the toys, such as eyes and smiles, you will need to know these basic stitches.

Duplicate stitch

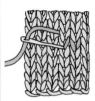

Straight stitch   **Couching stitch**

10. Making a pompom

Refer to the pattern for the required pompom maker size. You can buy pompom makers at most craft stores or make one simply with a piece of cardboard – cut two circles and cut out centre circles to match the required measurements.

a. Thread a wool needle and then wrap the wool around the pompom maker, pulling the needle through the centre and over the top, until the maker is covered with wool.
b. Cutting around the circumference of the pompom maker, cut the wool.
c. Take another piece of wool; place it between the two circles and tie it firmly around the centre of the wool.
d. Remove the two circles and you have a pompom.

b.   **c.**

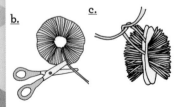

11. Making a tassel

Refer to the pattern for the required tassel maker size. All you need is a piece of cardboard around 10cm wide and as long as is required by the pattern.

a. Wind the wool around the cardboard 20-25 times, depending on how full (thick) you want the tassel to be.
b. Thread a wool needle with another piece of wool; insert this under all the wool at the top of the cardboard and then tie it firmly around all the wool.
c. Cut the wool at the bottom of the cardboard.
d. Wrap another piece of wool around the top of the tassel twice, to create the look of a small bobble at the top. Tie this tightly and then cut the ends so that they blend in with the rest of the ends of the tassel.

c.   **d.**

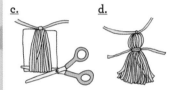

12. Knitting with two colours side-by-side

The penguin, bunny and shark patterns in this book require you to knit with two colours side by side. Here's how to do it to ensure that the two colours bind together:

a. Pick up the new wool beneath the dropped (previous) wool.
b. Wrap this new colour up and around the dropped wool as you go to knit the first stitch with the new colour.
c. Follow this process each time you switch colours.

a, b.

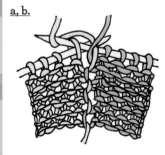

13. Mattress stitch

Vertical This stitch is used to join the edges of two pieces vertically.

a. Line up the edges of the pieces so that the stitches are all evenly next to each other.
b. Thread a wool needle with a new piece of wool; insert the wool needle under the horizontal strand between the first and second stitches of one side and the corresponding strand on the other side.
c. Insert the needle under the horizontal strand on the next row up then pull across and do the same on the other side.
d. Repeat this process, pulling every 6-10 stitches to tighten.

b, c, d.

Horizontal This stitch is used to join the edges of two pieces horizontally. In this book the horizontal mattress stitch is used for the top of the bunny ears and the penguin flippers, and the bottom of the shark fins. The method is exactly the same as for the vertical stitch, except you are inserting the needle under the "v" of the actual stitch instead of the horizontal strand between each of the stitches.

14. 3-needle joining

This creates one row of stitches from two rows.

a. Take the stitches and configure them across two parallel needles, ensuring there are an equal number of stitches across each needle.

b.

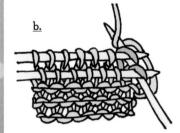

b. Simply knit through these two stitches at once as you would knit one stitch. When you bring the two stitches across to the opposite needle there will only be one stitch.
c. Repeat this until all stitches are on the opposite needle in one row.

When instructed to use this method to attach an arm or leg, and it is too challenging, you can join and then cast-off your row of stitches instead (see below, '3-needle joining and binding') and then sew your piece onto the body.

15. 3-needle joining and binding

The robot, dinosaur and giraffe patterns in this book require you to use this method to completely close off the top of the work to create an edge.

a. Knit two stitches following the steps of 3-needle joining.
b. Once you have these two stitches on the opposite needle, pull the first one over the second, exactly as you would if you were casting off.
c. Repeat this process until all the stitches are cast off.

16. French knitting (spool knitting)

French knitting dollies can be purchased, but it's quite easy to make your own. If you are going to purchase one for the purpose of this book, you will need one with a 15-20mm diameter. The diameter dictates how large and loose the stitches will be.

Making the dolly
a. Take a toilet paper roll and cut a straight line down the length to open it up.
b. Roll it into a tight tube, so that the diameter is around 15-20mm; sticky tape the seam closed tightly.
c. Take 4 x 4mm double-pointed needles and tape them evenly around the roll as if to make a square. You are done!

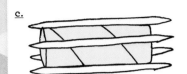
<u>c.</u>

French knitting technique
a. Take the wool end and insert it into the top of the French knitting dolly – drop it down until it just hangs out the bottom. Let this hang – this is like the cast on end and you just let it drop. The wool attached to the ball is known as the working wool.
b. With the dolly in your left hand (right hand if you are left-handed) and the wool in the right (left) hand, take the wool and wrap it counter-clockwise around the first needle.
c. Moving the wool counter-clockwise across the top, wrap the wool counter-clockwise around the next needle. Complete this process until all needles have two loops.
d. Using a crochet hook (or if you are really nimble, your fingers), pull each bottom loop over the top loop.
e. Continue to wrap the wool counter-clockwise around each needle in a counter-clockwise pattern, finishing whenever you have two rows of loops; pull the bottom loop over the top.
f. To finish, simply cut the working end, thread a wool needle and then pull the end through all of the loops on the dolly.

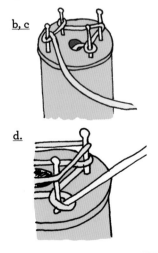
<u>b, c</u>

<u>d.</u>

17. Strand knitting (Fair Isle)
This style of knitting is only used in the giraffe pattern in this book to create his spots. Strand knitting refers to switching backwards and forwards between two or more colours in the same row.

a. Drop the wool colour you are knitting with.
b. Pick up the new colour and simply loop it around the next stitch.
c. As the pattern dictates, drop this and pick up the new colour.
d. Depending on how many stitches there are between colours there will be a strand that you carry across when you need to knit with the new colour. Ensure that you leave a fair amount of slack when you pull across the wool to knit – if you pull too tightly you will bunch the work.
e. If you notice the wools becoming tangled, rest assured, this is a common occurrence, as you are wrapping the wools around each other as you switch colours. We recommend that you untangle after each row to keep the work manageable.

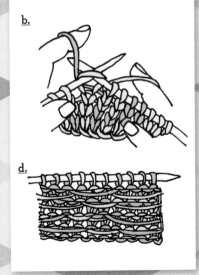
b.

d.

HELPFUL HINTS

1. Using a stitch holder

Standard stitch holders look like giant safety pins – it is where you can put your stitches when you are not knitting them. It can be tricky to put stitches that are in a circular configuration onto one straight holder. We transfer our circular stitches onto a holder with the following steps:

a. Lay your work flat with the needles parallel to one another – one in the front and two in the back.
b. Using the stitch holder, take one stitch from alternating needles so that you are closing off the top (you are unable to knit into these stitches while they remain on the stitch holder).
c. When transferring your work back onto the needles, start by taking two parallel needles, as you slip the stitches off the holder, place on alternate needles as you go so that your work opens up (once you transfer the stitches back onto the needles, you are now able to knit into these stitches).
d. Once your work is on two needles, reconfigure the stitches across 3 needles as the pattern requires.

<u>**b.**</u>

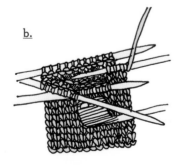

2. Joining new wool or changing colours

If you run out of wool, your wool breaks or your pattern requires you to change to a new colour, you will need to join new wool.

a. Ensure that you don't knit right to the end of your wool – leave around 15cm hanging.
b. Simply knit the next stitch with your new wool, looping the new wool around the needle with around 15cm hanging loose.
c. Tie a loose knot to join these two ends together.

3. Sewing onto your work

Sewing with knitted pieces is the same principle as hand sewing with regular fabric – only everything is a bit thicker. We recommend using the same colour wool as the piece you are sewing on and a series of straight stitches (see page 114, *'embroidery stitches - straight stitch'*) just inside the edge of the piece you are attaching.

Sew any embellishments (faces, ears, flippers, etc) onto your work after it is completed and stuffed, as stuffing may stretch the stitches a bit; this way your attaching will be more accurate.
Use the loose end of your work to sew – if you haven't left enough wool, weave in a new strand (see *weaving method to hide wool ends*, right). When you are finished, hide the loose end inside the body (see *'hiding wool inside of body'*, right).

4. Hiding wool inside of body

a. Thread the needle with the wool you want to hide.
b. Poke the needle with the wool inside the body and firmly pull needle with wool still threaded to the outside.
c. Cut this wool very close to the body and it will spring back inside.

5. Weaving method to hide wool ends

If you find yourself with loose wool ends that you can't easily hide, you can weave them into the back of your work. This will be particularly helpful for hiding the ends of the shark's teeth.

a. Thread a wool needle with the loose wool end.
b. Insert the needle up into the back of two to three stitches, then loop back around and insert down through two to three stitches.
c. If you have space you can repeat this a few times. For the shark teeth you will only have space to do this twice.
d. Cut the loose end close to your work, leaving around a 5mm end.

<u>**b.**</u>

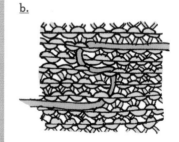

Here are some hints that will help you fix common problems and make your finished work a bit more polished.

6. Sewing on pompoms and tassels

Many of the patterns in this book use pompoms or tassels to create embellishments on the body.

You need to sew the pompoms and tassels on very tightly – especially if you are planning on giving your knitted toy to a young child or curious adult.

a. Use the loose ends from tying the pompom/tassel together to sew them onto the toy. We recommend leaving a 30cm minimum length.
b. Thread a wool needle with one end of the wool.
c. Insert the needle into the toy where you want to place the pompom/tassel, pulling out it three horizontal stitches away.
d. Pull the wool through and back out the centre of the pompom/tassel, where all the wool is tied together.
e. Repeat this process multiple times to secure – we did 8 loops for a pompom.
f. Cut the end and hide it in the pompom/tassel when you are done.
g. Repeat this process with the second loose end.

7. Fixing a slipped stitch

A slipped stitch is easy to do and let go unnoticed but, fortunately, it isn't too hard to fix!

a. With the right side facing, insert a crochet hook into the slipped stitch.
b. Push the hook up further and hook it on to the top of the strand of wool in the row above the slipped stitch.
c. With the hook, pull this strand through the loop below it.
d. Repeat this process until the stitch has made its way back to the top of the work. Then you can simply place it back on the needle.

a, b, c.

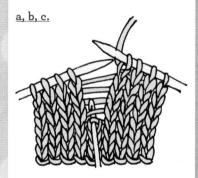

To avoid slipping a stitch, be mindful of the stitch count for each round/row – it is easier to notice a missing stitch if you are always aware of how many stitches you should have on the needle.

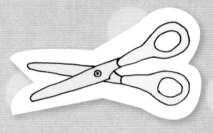

8. Laddering

Laddering is a term that refers to a gap that can form between needles when knitting in the round.

This is a common occurrence – even experienced knitters can get a bit of a laddering. The only way to minimise this gap is to knit the first couple of stitches on each needle very firmly.

To help minimise the appearance of a ladder on your finished work:

a. Take a piece of wool that is at least twice the length of the ladder.
b. Thread a wool needle and weave it through the outside loop of each stitch on either side of the ladder.
c. Once you have weaved through the entire ladder, pull on either end of the strand so your work slightly bunches together. Hold this for a few seconds, and repeat a few times.
d. Pull the wool out. You will notice that the ladder has closed a little.

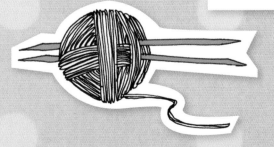

INDEX

First published in 2013 by Bauer Media Books, a division of Bauer Media Ltd,
54 Park St, Sydney; GPO Box 4088, Sydney, NSW 2001.
Phone (02) 9282 8618; fax (02) 9126 3702.

Publishing director Gerry Reynolds
Publisher Sally Wright
Pattern development and knitter Karla Courtney
Editorial director Pamela Clark
Sales & rights director Brian Cearnes
Creative director Hieu Chi Nguyen
Art director & designer Hannah Blackmore

This edition published in 2014 by Bounty Books
a division of Octopus Publishing Group Ltd

Endeavour House, 189 Shaftesbury Avenue, London WC2H 8JY

www.octopusbooks.co.uk

An Hachette UK Company

www.hachette.co.uk

Copyright © Bauer Media Ltd 2013
ABN 18 053 273 546

A catalogue record for this book is available from the British Library.
ISBN: 978 0 75372 859 8

Printed and bound in Thailand